Christmas 2016

Dean Cath,

GOD IS NOT FAIR,
and Other Reasons for Gratitude

DANIEL P. HORAN, OFM

*With Love
always,
Dan* ♡

Franciscan
MEDIA
Cincinnati, Ohio

Cover design by LUCAS Art & Design
Book design by Mark Sullivan

LIBRARY OF CONGRESS CATALOGING-IN-PUBLICATION DATA
Names: Horan, Daniel P., author.
Title: God is not fair, and other reasons for gratitude / Daniel P. Horan, OFM.
Description: Cincinnati : Franciscan Media, 2016.
Identifiers: LCCN 2016026608 | ISBN 9781632531414 (trade paper)
Subjects: LCSH: Christian life—Catholic authors. | God—Impartiality. | Providence and government of God—Christianity. | Christianity and culture—Biblical teaching. | Vocation—Catholic Church. | Francis, of Assisi, Saint, 1182-1226.
Classification: LCC BX2350.3 .H67 2016 | DDC 248.4/82—dc23
LC record available at https://lccn.loc.gov/2016026608
ISBN 978-1-63253-141-4

Published by Franciscan Media
28 W. Liberty St.
Cincinnati, OH 45202
www.FranciscanMedia.org

Printed in the United States of America.
Printed on acid-free paper.
16 17 18 19 20 5 4 3 2 1

To Jessica Coblentz,
whose friendship is yet another reason for gratitude

Contents

Introduction

GOD IS NOT FAIR. ALTHOUGH THIS STATEMENT may strike some readers as disrespectful or at least odd, the truth is that the title of this book is 100 percent correct. It is an uncomfortable fact, a reality that is made clear by Jesus Christ himself and by everything that has been handed on to us about his life, death, and resurrection. Christians profess belief in the reality that what we see and know in Christ we see and know of God. John's Gospel begins with this affirmation in the prologue (John 1:18), the opening lines of the Letter to the Hebrews restates this truth (Hebrews 1:1–4), and yet so often, we ignore the fullness of God's revelation in Christ and instead construct fair gods in our world's image and likeness. We do our own thing, see our own perspective, and demand that others follow our way of being—all the while calling these things "God's will."

That God is not fair is actually one among many reasons for gratitude, albeit in a way counterintuitive to our usual thinking. The simple premise here is that God's way is not our way, God's love is not conditioned like our love, God's mercy is not bound as ours is, and God does not discriminate or reward a person according to the standards of a given society, no matter how widespread such criteria may be. (Thank God!) As I explain in detail later in this book, God's lack of fairness by human standards should challenge us to reconsider not how capricious or malicious God is, but rather how inappropriate, unchristian, and inhumane we are. It seems to me that too much of our faith is governed by our own insecurities, self-interests, and fears. And yet, often we project what we see of our world, justified through the lenses of worldly logic, onto others and into our religion as if it were not our way, but God's way.

This book is a series of short reflections that takes as its starting point a belief that we must consider our faith at the intersection of theology, Scripture, and culture and do so with a willingness to see with new eyes, think with open minds, and care with loving hearts. The result, I hope, is an increase of reasons for gratitude.

The chapters are organized into three parts. The first part focuses on the promise and challenge of Christian faith in the modern world. I believe, like St. Paul long before me, that what we profess as Christian women and men is foolishness to the world that demands a kind of unjust logic. What, then, does our faith look like when it is confronted by the pressures, temptations, challenges, and everyday realities of our modern lives? How do we follow Christ in our contemporary setting? And can we refresh our vision and renew our experience of prayer, worship, and daily life? These are the themes that open this book.

The second part is centered on the relationship between sacred Scripture and our contemporary culture. These reflections take seriously the meaning of the Bible as inspired by the Holy Spirit and as passed on by generations of faithful believers. It is my hope that with each chapter, you may gain at least one new insight about our sacred texts. However, it is not enough to know the history or meaning of the Bible. Christians believe that Scripture is alive and the Spirit continues to speak to the hearts of women and men in each generation and at all times. With this in mind, I invite you to explore with me the possibility that God continues to speak to us today, discomfiting the complacent and reassuring the anxious, the depressed, and the despairing.

The last part of this book shifts gears to consider our understanding of vocation. Usually when we hear the word *vocation*, we think of priests and nuns, professed religious and preachers, and yet the term is expansive enough to include all baptized believers. From the day we were incorporated into the Body of Christ in baptism, each of us received a call to follow Jesus Christ by living the Gospel. The reflections in this part of the book are offered as a starting point for reimagining what it means to talk about Christian living in whatever state of life we find ourselves.

At the end of Francis of Assisi's life, he is remembered to have said to his brother friars, "The Lord has shown me what was mine to do in this life, may the Lord show you what is yours." The spirit of this book is not to offer an absolute answer to all the particular questions that may arise in your efforts to follow the Gospel and grow as a human being in community. Instead, these reflections are presented to you in the spirit of St. Francis's parting words. These are insights, challenges, and invitations that I share from my experience and reflection in the hope that they might ignite within your heart further consideration of the many ways God continues to speak to your own life and encourage you to follow in the footprints of Jesus Christ.

PART I

Following Christ in the Modern World

AT TIMES, THERE CAN SEEM TO BE A BIG disconnect between the time of Jesus Christ and his early followers and the world in which we find ourselves today. It was a simpler time, we might have thought on occasion when hearing about Jesus's difficult instructions to his followers. We may consider our world and circumstances so different from those of the first followers of Christ that we excuse ourselves from the challenge of loving enemies, forgiving those who harm us, or caring for the poor and marginalized in our midst.

Still, at other times, we may feel so confused about what we are meant to do or how God wants us to live that we simply shrug our shoulders and just go on doing what we've been doing anyway. It is almost certainly easier to give up than to wrestle with the hard things in faith and life.

If there's one thing that can be said about trying to be a Christian—today or at any time, for that matter—it's that it is not easy. If God's message to us in Jesus Christ was easy or comfortable, chances are he wouldn't have been seen as the threat that he was to the status quo and therefore executed. To be a Christian is to be a radical like Christ. *Radical* here does not mean a fanatic or self-righteous individual, but *radical* in the original sense of the term from the Latin *radix*, which means "root." Christians believe that God entered the world as one of us to teach us what it means to be fully human, to challenge us to return to the roots of authentic human life and society, and to show us the way to love one another as God loves us.

Navigating the complexities and distractions of our increasingly busy lives, especially those who live in the technology-saturated land of the United States, may require from us new skills and disciplines, but the basic

1

foundation of Christian living remains as relevant as it is ancient. The essays in this first section are reflections on the intersection of faith and life, explorations about where the ancient past and the modern present meet. What does it mean to return to the roots of our Christian faith? How do we follow Christ in the modern world? These are the guiding questions for the challenging considerations that follow.

CONTRARY TO POPULAR OPINION, I think it's sometimes good to be a fool. Allow me to explain.

Most people approach foolishness in one of two ways. The first is to avoid any such scenario at all costs because the specter of failure and embarrassment haunts our professional, emotional, and social lives, quietly tempering us from sharing opinions or speaking up in front of others. The second is to exploit one's potential foolishness to an extreme degree. While those who wish to avoid appearing foolish might recoil at the thought of public humiliation, in stark contrast, people every day rise as stars of YouTube, reality television, and daytime talk shows by acting as foolish as possible.

Neither of these approaches offers a satisfactory illustration of what I have in mind. What I have in mind is what could be called "evangelical foolishness" or the act of becoming "God's fool," a term that has been applied to St. Francis of Assisi. Francis might rightly be regarded as the patron saint of fools. He offers us a surprising, if uneasy, Christian virtue between two foolish vices.

The very core of Christianity appears foolish to the world. Take, for instance, the idea that God would become human. At the heart of Christian faith stands the radical idea that the all-powerful God would bow low to enter creation as a vulnerable infant. Or take the doctrine of the Trinity; mathematically, the claim that God is at the same time one and yet three divine persons appears laughable to many. Or take the love and mercy of God: As Pope Francis has reiterated from the beginning of his ministry as bishop of Rome, God's mercy and love are unconditional. In a world where one is often encouraged to return insult with insult, pain with pain, the ministry and example of Jesus Christ make little sense.

This sense of Christian foolishness was a truth that St. Paul recognized early in his ministry to first-century Gentiles, who could not easily reconcile the God of Jesus Christ with the Hellenistic worldview they otherwise held (1 Corinthians 1:23). The expectations of their time and culture did not smoothly align with the preaching of the incarnate Word or the cruci-fied and risen Christ. Likewise, the ethical implications of the words and deeds of Jesus for those disciples that would follow him were not always in step with the standard practices and behaviors of their day, just as they aren't always easily compatible with those of our time.

This is where evangelical foolishness comes into play. Francis earned the title because of his allegiance to the Gospel over the culture of his rearing. He refused to accept money in the newly emerging merchant society because he saw how this nascent economic and social system began valuing people according to their wealth. He refused in other ways to participate in the power imbalances of his day because he recognized that following in the footprints of Christ meant prioritizing solidarity and relationships with all people rather than pursuing the accumulation of personal wealth and power.

Francis's commitment to this way of being in the world, what he would call the *vita evangelica* ("Gospel life") appeared foolish to his peers in Assisi. He was at first mocked for his new lifestyle and commitments. Francis was a certain type of fool, a fool whose life and actions revealed Gospel wisdom.

I have often heard some of my Franciscan brothers say, "If Francis had applied to religious life today, he'd never make it beyond the psychological exam!" How true that is! (You should see that exam.) Even retrospectively, Francis is dismissed as a madman.

The risk of appearing foolish never stopped him from embracing the Gospel as best he could, protesting the injustices of certain social systems, and letting nothing get in the way of his relationship with others. The virtue between the two foolish vices of avoidance and exploitation is the embrace of evangelical foolishness to become one of God's fools. But as Paul makes clear to the Corinthians, being a Christian means those very things: appearing mad, foolish, and out-of-step with the rest of society at times. This is because a Christian's priorities aren't measured by popular culture, but according to the reign of God (*Basileia tou Theou*) that Jesus preached and modeled. It is the counterintuitive and gratuitous foolish-ness of God's love revealed in the healing of the broken and brokenhearted, forgiving the unforgiveable, and loving the unlovable.

So becoming a fool for God's sake isn't something to avoid out of fear or exploit for personal gain, but a vocation to embrace in revealing the love of God in our lives. I challenge you—and remind myself all the time—to consider why, where, and how to be a fool for Christ.

Zombies are everywhere! At least that is what our contemporary cinematic and popular literary market would have us believe. With the current onslaught of the undead through the various platforms of video games, comedy, books, film, and even spoofed classic literature (for example, Pride and Prejudice and Zombies, as well as its many spinoffs and imitations), zombies have infiltrated our cultural psyche in a way that is rivaled only by the popularity of their more seductive supernatural cousins, the vampires.

A few years back, Jack McLain wrote a thoughtful piece in America about the cultural significance of the increasing zombie attack and mentioned the then-recent publication of Max Brook's book World War Z, which was released as a film a few years later.[1] While zombies aren't typically my thing, I saw the movie in no small part because of the surprisingly positive review offered by the New Yorker's film critic David Denby, who asserted, "World War Z is the most gratifying action spectacle in years."[2] Who could pass up that opportunity?

Seeing World War Z was enough to elicit in me an unexpected interest in the cultural phenomenon of recent zombie popularity. Why was it so pervasive, and why I had succumbed to being bitten by this mythic monster?

There has been a lot of reflection in recent years on the social criticism in the zombie genre that isn't as obvious in some other supernatural or mythical methods of storytelling. These considerations include society's obsession with unbridled consumption to a psychoanalytic reading of the zombie as a nonliving specter of Freud's theory of the death drive haunting our collective desire for control and meaning. I think these and other theories are compelling and helpful, but as someone particularly interested in theology and spirituality, I am more drawn to what the cultural obsession with the undead might say about our faith.

What is most frightening about zombies, theologian Kim Praffenroth

1. Jack McClain, "A Need to Feed: What zombies tell us about our culture," *America*, May 17, 2010.
2. David Denby, "Life and Undeath," *The New Yorker,* July 1, 2013.

observes in an excellent book, Gospel of the Living Dead, is that, "unlike aliens, robots, or supernatural beings, such as demons, the distasteful and horrible aspects of zombies cannot really be discounted as unhuman, but are rather just exaggerated aspects of humanity."[3] Zombies don't embody an enemy from without, but as another theologian explains in a recent article, "zombies represent the alien within us."[4]

Classic zombie films such as those by George Romero typically portray the surviving nonzombie humans as scrambling to respond to the effects of the zombie attack rather than address its causes. Likewise, the means to address the effects tend to be individualistic and violent. Not only do the zombies reveal us at our worst, but the behavior of the surviving humans do as well.

What is interesting about World War Z is that both of these characteristics are eventually reversed. The story focuses on the quest to find the cause of this outbreak, which leads the protagonist around the world. In addressing the root of the problem, a violent defense proves useless, and weakness saves the lives of those who survive. Religion News Service blogger Jana Reiss recognized something Christlike here: "Weakness becomes strength. Actively choosing weakness—especially when every cell of your body is screaming to cling to power instead—leads to life. Huh. That sounds a whole lot like Jesus."[5]

If we look at the compulsive, consumptive, individualistic, and violent aspects of the undead and those who fight them as an allegory for our human sinfulness, the zombie genre might rightly serve as a reminder of what it means to have real life, and to have it to the fullest. What makes us "a whole lot like Jesus" is when we address the causes and not just the effects of systemic sin in our world, like poverty or violence, when we embrace community rather than succumb to the temptation to care only for ourselves, and when we actively choose weakness and humility rather than defending our desire for control, power, and security. So if it's true

---

3. Kim Paffenroth, Gospel of the Living Dead: George Romero's Vision of Hell on Earth (Waco, TX: Baylor University Press, 2006), 11.
4. See Ola Sigurdson, "Slavoj Zizek, the Death Drive, and Zombies: A Theological Account," Modern Theology 29 (2013): 361–380.
5. Jana Riess, "Finding God in World War Z," RNS Blog, July 17, 2013.

that zombies serve to remind us of what lurks deep within ourselves, then perhaps the stories about resisting them also offer us cautionary tales of how not to be human when trying to overcome our worst selves.

I HAVE JUST RECENTLY TURNED THIRTY. While that seemed somewhat old to me as I approached the milestone, most people were quick to remind me of how young a friar and priest I still was. That statement of fact—my relative youth—is often but not always accompanied by some well-meaning remark by a parishioner after Mass or an audience member after a talk suggesting that I'm not like other young priests they know.

What generally follows that sort of comment is an expression of concern about the perceived unapproachable or pretentious character of so many of the newly ordained. They talk about men who appear to be more concerned about titles, clerical attire, and fancy vestments, who distance themselves from their parishioners, and who focus more on what makes them distinctive than the vocation that they have received to wash the feet of another (John 13:14–17), to lead with humility, and to show the compassionate face of God to all. In other words, the concern is with clericalism.

What I hear in these moments is not a compliment or praise, but the worry people have for the future of ministry and the Church. As St. Francis of Assisi cautioned his brothers, I realize that anything good that comes from my work as a priest is God's work, and the only things I can truly take credit for are my weaknesses and sinfulness, and trust me, there are plenty of both in my life. St. Francis explains this idea to his brother friars in Admonition V, in which he says that we can take no credit for the good works God does through us, "but we can boast in our weaknesses and in carrying each day the holy cross of our Lord Jesus Christ."[1] At the heart of any encounters I have as a priest with God's people is the intuitive recognition that we are all sinners, yet we all have equal dignity as the baptized, and those ordained to the ministerial priesthood should serve their sisters and brothers on our journey of faith. And many don't.

---

1. Francis of Assisi, "Admonition V," v. 8, in *Francis of Assisi: Early Documents*, eds. Regis J. Armstrong, J.A. Wayne Hellmann, and William J. Short, vol. 1 (New York: New City, 1999), 131. All future quotes from the writings of St. Francis are taken from this edition.

While I know many good and humble religious and diocesan priests, I've also encountered far too many clergy who, for whatever reason, feel they are above, better, or more special than others. Pope Francis has, of course, helped to change this enormously since being elected bishop of Rome in the spring of 2013. He recognizes this reality and spoke critically about it, for instance, on the impromptu plane ride interview after World Youth Day. *Catholic News Service* reported:

> "I think this is a time for mercy," particularly a time when the church must go out of its way to be merciful given the "not-so-beautiful witness of some priests" and "the problem of clericalism, for example, which have left so many wounds, so many wounded. The church, which is mother, must go and heal those wounds."[2]

The pope names this culture of clericalism that maims and distorts the body of Christ, wounding those who seek God's mercy but encounter human self-centeredness.

Again, in an extended interview published in *America*, Pope Francis suggested ministers could help heal these wounds with mercy. He said, "The most important thing is the first proclamation: Jesus Christ has saved you. And the ministers of the church must be ministers of mercy above all."[3]

St. Francis of Assisi is often remembered for having had a special reverence for priests, a characteristic that appears frequently in his writings. But he also had a particular vision for how the brothers in his community, ordained or not, would live in the world. His instruction seems as timely as ever in light of the persistence of clericalism. In his Earlier Rule, Francis says, "Let no one be called 'prior,' but let everyone in general be called a lesser brother." He also wrote in Admonition XIX:

> Blessed is the servant who does not consider himself any better when he is praised and exalted by people than when he is considered worthless, simple, and looked down upon, for what a person is

2. Cindy Wooden, "Pope discusses women in the church, divorce, his own spirituality," *Catholic News Service*, July 29, 2013, http://www.catholicnews.com/services/english-news/2013/pope-discusses-women-in-the-church-divorce-his-own-spirituality.cfm.
3. Pope Francis, "A Big Heart Open to God," *America*, September 30, 2013.

before God, that he is and no more. Woe to that religious who has been placed in a high position by others and [who] does not want to come down by his own will. Blessed is that servant who is not placed in a high position by his own will and always desired to be under the feet of others.[4]

All clergy, not just Franciscans, should be challenged by these words. I know that I am.

We are now a few years into Pope Francis's pontificate, and I sense that he will continue to challenge the whole Church, especially its ordained members, to a Christian way of servant leadership. As a part of this, his call for humbler and more generous priests is a call to work against a culture of clericalism. It is a call so there never have to be awkward post-Mass conversations like the ones I sometimes experience. It is a call for priests and bishops, young and old, to remember that their baptism is what matters most.

---

4. Francis of Assisi, Admonition XIX, FA:ED, vol. 1, 135.

SITTING IN A CAMBRIDGE, MASSACHUSETTS, movie theater with a friend, I forced myself not to look or shy away from the violent scenes in Steve McQueen's *12 Years a Slave*. Unlike the gratuitous violence of Mel Gibson's *The Passion of the Christ* or Quentin Tarantino's *Django Unchained*, there was nothing over-the-top, nothing selfish about what was painfully depicted on screen in McQueen's adaptation of the story of Solomon Northup. That is what made it so difficult to watch and why I wanted to look away so badly. The presentation seemed so real.

As Yale historian David Blight, an expert on American slavery, said in an NPR interview, "We love being the country that freed the slaves, [but] we're not so fond of being the country that had the biggest slave system on the planet."[1] Whereas Gibson's depiction of the Passion was an idiosyncratic reflection of his own personal piety and Tarantino's slave film was fictive, *12 Years a Slave* offers an indicting narrative that forces its viewers—particularly its white American viewers—to confront a dangerous memory that we would collectively like to forget.

Blight said that the history of American slavery is "a problem in our culture because, to be quite blunt about it, most Americans want their history to be essentially progressive and triumphal, they want it to be a pleasing story. And if you go back to this story, it's not always going to please you, but it's a story you have to work through to find your way to something more redemptive."

The way Blight talked about the importance of McQueen's film reminded me of the work of German theologian Johann Baptist Metz. In his book *Faith in History and Society*, Metz describes two types of memories. The first is the sterilized form of memory "in which we just do not take the past seriously enough" and recall everything in a soft, glowing light. This type of memory is usually evolutionary or progressive, reflecting a trajectory of history moving toward an increasingly better world. The other type is what

---

1. "Historian Says '12 Years' Is a Story the Nation Must Remember," *Fresh Air*, NPR, October 12, 2013.

Metz calls "dangerous memories, memories which make demands on us." The latter are what he sees as constituting the Christian narrative when we take seriously the life, death, and resurrection of Jesus Christ. Metz explains that these dangerous memories "illuminate for a few moments and with a harsh steady light the questionable nature of things we have apparently come to terms with, and show up the banality of our supposed 'realism.'"[2]

Far too often, the history of slavery in the United States is reduced to the sterile, clichéd, and comforting former type of memory. The stark reality of slavery and our collective complicity in its perpetuation is reduced to a caricature. Alternatively, we tell a story about the triumphant work of liberator and martyr Abraham Lincoln and the Civil War, which overshadows the complexity of a past marred by the indescribable suffering of generations of persons that had been dehumanized, sold, owned, raped, murdered, and destroyed. Many who have the luxury to look away and forget, do. This is a selective memory that silences the oppressed, the victims, and the dead. This is a kind of memory that allows the sins of American racism and white privilege to continue today, an unquestioned status quo shielded by our willful ignorance and desire for so-called historical progress.

But slavery in this nation is a memory of the latter kind, a dangerous memory. Like the resurrection of Christ, which can never be separated from his life and death, there is something redeeming about the calling to mind the suffering caused by American slavery and its continuing effects. What is redemptive isn't the belief that all is OK now. Rather, the way toward redemption is directed by an awareness that things are far from OK. What makes the memory of American slavery so dangerous is that, in calling to mind the suffering of history's victims, we begin to see that the suffering continues. Hope is found in the interruption that films like *12 Years a Slave* make in our everyday lives and presumptions. This interruption should shock us into hearing the muted cries of history's victims (Psalm 34) and recall that, although we are many parts, we are one body in Christ (1 Corinthians 12:12).

---

2. Johann Baptist Metz, *Faith in History and Society: Toward a Practical Fundamental Theology*, trans. J. Matthew Ashley (New York: Crossroad, 2011), 105–106.

The body of Christ continues to suffer. The dangerous memory of slavery calls us to take seriously the question: What are you and I going to do about it?

ON DECEMBER 10, 2013, THE EYES, ears, and hearts of the world were focused on Soweto, South Africa, on the occasion of a memorial service to remember the life and legacy of Nelson Mandela. Mandela will be remembered for a great many things, including his commitment to peacemaking and nonviolence in his later years. However, in a way unlike Dr. Martin Luther King Jr. or Mahatma Gandhi, with whom Mandela will be remembered as a great world leader of liberation, Mandela's relationship to nonviolence and peacemaking was especially complex.

In the *Los Angeles Times* in the days leading up to the memorial service, Robyn Dixon reminded us how Mandela once "embraced armed struggle to end the racist system of apartheid." In the 1950s and 1960s, Mandela was convinced that the nonviolent efforts the African National Congress (ANC) had adopted to fight the white supremacist regime were ineffectual. He and others trained for military action and established Umkhonto we Sizwe, the armed branch of the ANC, which was willing to use violence to reach its goals. Yet, this was not the stance Mandela would always maintain.

Dixon goes on to explain how "Umkhonto we Sizwe abandoned its policy of violence in 1990 as negotiations on the dismantling of apartheid and the setting up of free elections continued. After his release, and on becoming South Africa's chief executive in 1994, Mandela adhered to the commitment to peace, tolerance and equality that became the hallmark of his presidency."[1]

Although his story isn't about embracing radical nonviolence from the outset, Mandela's story is about conversion to nonviolence. His is a story that offers hope for those who believe that they cannot let go of the necessity of violence in our world. His is a story that encourages us, especially those who bear the name of Christ, to give nonviolence a chance.

Nonviolence is often viewed as impossible and seen as an unrealistic dream of the naïve and foolish, particularly in an age marked by drones,

---

1. Robyn Dixon, "Nelson Mandela's Legacy: As a Leader, He was willing to use Violence," *Los Angeles Times*, December 6, 2013.

nuclear weapons, and diffuse terrorism networks. This sort of logic is what led the young Mandela to endorse taking up arms.

However, there are prophets that continue to cry out in the wilderness of our twenty-first–century world on behalf of nonviolence. For example, Pope Francis called Christians and all people of good will to join him in a prayer vigil for peace in Syria on September 7, 2013. During that day of prayer and fasting, Pope Francis spoke at St. Peter's Square: "We have perfected our weapons, our conscience has fallen asleep, and we have sharpened our ideas to justify ourselves as if it were normal we continue to sow destruction, pain, death. Violence and war lead only to death." The pope, who has been nominated for the Nobel Peace Prize by the Argentinean government for this nonviolent witness and its result, was offering a challenge to the world to follow in the spirit of Mandela's own lifelong conversion toward peace and nonviolence.

What seems impossible and illogical might just be our own unwillingness to take seriously the Gospel imperative of peace. Pope Francis asked during the peace vigil: "Can we get out of this spiral of sorrow and death? Can we learn once again to walk and live in the ways of peace?" And offered a Gospel response: "I say yes it is possible for everyone. From every corner of the world tonight, I would like to hear us cry out: Yes, it is possible for everyone!" His challenge to us is to return to the Gospel and embrace nonviolence as the way to be peacemakers and reconcilers. Nelson Mandela's life story illustrates the possibility of this conversion. The logic of violence has had its reign for long enough. Can we too give nonviolence a chance?

Were you there when they Crucified my Lord?
Were you there when they Crucified my Lord?
Oh, OOOoohh, sometimes it causes me to Tremble, Tremble, Tremble.
Were you there when they Crucified my Lord?

Were you there when they Crucified Cecil Clayton?
Were you there when they Crucified Manuel Vasquez?
Oh, OOOoohh, always, it should cause us to Tremble, Tremble, Tremble.
Were you there when they Crucified Walter Storey?

Or Donald Newbury or Robert Ladd or Warren Hill or Arnold Prieto or Charles Frederick Warner or Johnny Kormondy or Andrew Brannan or Roderick Nunley or Alfredo Rolando Prieto? These are the names of just thirteen of the human beings that the government by the people, of the people, and for the people in this country has recently executed.

What we commemorate on Good Friday is a state execution, the death of a man who was viewed as a threat to those in religious and civil authority, a man who was executed by the Romans for what was considered "the fomenting of insurrection." We just hear the proceedings and we recognize the charge in the Gospel reading on that day. (You might take ten minutes and slowly read John 18:1—19:42.)

While we may honestly say that we were not there when they crucified our Lord, we have to ask ourselves on this day when torture, capital punishment, and the death of innocents is front and center: Does the perpetuation of the injustice of the death penalty in our country cause us to tremble, tremble, tremble?

It should!

I've been fortunate to live for years, now, in the commonwealth of Massachusetts, a state that has, since October 18, 1984, banned the death penalty. But recently, down the street at the federal court house in Boston, the US government—in my name and that of so many others—ruled to take yet another human life, that of convicted Boston Marathon bomber

Dzhokhar Tsarnaev. If on Good Friday you don't think about Dzhokhar (or any of the many other people who are still on death row), then I believe you're missing a big part of the picture. The whole celebration of this holy day for Christians is a commemoration, a calling to mind of the state execution of God-made-human.

One of the big temptations of Good Friday is to confuse feeling sorry or sorrowful with feeling sorry for oneself! This, for example, is what Mel Gibson's film *The Passion of the Christ* so often perpetuates. It was drawn not from good scriptural exegesis or sound theology, but from the gruesome visions of a German nun, whose written idea of what happened on Calvary is what the director primarily used in that film. The effect, and if you've seen it you know, is to play on the emotions that arise from watching obscene torture, to make individuals feel horrified and bad.

This is not what the crucifixion of our Lord is about! This is not why Jesus was executed!

Taking Good Friday as an opportunity to dwell on how bad we are such that we stay in the realm of feeling sorry for ourselves is not the point. Instead, yes, we should—on Good Friday and always—reflect on how we need to repent for the wrong we've done and the right we have failed to do, but then we are, like Jesus after falling for the first, second, and third times, called by God to get up and move forward!

Pope Francis has talked a lot about Good Friday and the death penalty during his powerful term as Bishop of Rome. He has asked us in his apostolic exhortation The Joy of the Gospel to consider whether or not we are "Christians whose lives seem like Lent without Easter." Whether we, in other words, use this time of penance, prayer, and conversion to feel sorry for ourselves, to go around mopey or gloomy, to be a burden for others, or whether we move toward the joy of Easter, the joy which proclaims that indeed death and sin do not have the last word.

In terms of capital punishment, the Holy Father included a reflection on the injustice of the death penalty in his own recent Good Friday meditations on the Stations of the Cross—by calling us to work toward ending this evil in our world. It is no accident that he also spends every Lord's Supper evening celebrating the liturgy with prisoners and washing their feet. This is a modeling of the way of love to which Jesus calls all of us.

Recently, while meeting with a delegation of the International Commission Against the Death Penalty, Pope Francis said that "capital punishment is cruel, inhumane and degrading, and that it does not bring justice to the victims, but only foments revenge." You and I, as we follow the Lord along the way of the cross, bearing witness to the state execution of the Word made flesh, should ask ourselves: What good does the death penalty do?

Seriously, what good does it accomplish? What grace, what healing, what contribution to human flourishing does it bring about?

It only brings about more evil. The murder of someone is always still murder—to deliberately take another human life is always wrong, no matter who pulls the trigger or pushes the poison in the syringe.

Similarly, Pope Francis said, "The death penalty is an affront to the sanctity of life and to the dignity of the human person, it contradicts God's plan for humankind and society and God's merciful justice."

Many Christians fancy themselves as being pro-life, by which they typically mean that they are anti-abortion. Many of these same Christians claim that the difference between abortion and capital punishment is innocence. The unborn somehow have an innocent human life, but the inmate on death row has some other kind of life. But the Gospel and Christ make it clear: All human life is innocent! To say that we have inherent dignity and value as created and loved into existence by God means that there is nothing that can take that away from us. As Sr. Helen Prejean, the death penalty activist and author of *Dead Man Walking*, frequently says, "We are all more than the worst things we've done!"

This does not excuse horrendous and tragic behaviors, crimes, and actions—no, those things certainly merit punishment. But to say that a woman or man convicted of a crime has somehow lost their right to live is to take God's judgment into our own hands.

The late archbishop of Chicago, Cardinal Joseph Bernadin, was a tireless voice for the Christian pro-life movement—he advocated for what is called the seamless garment doctrine, which means that you cannot pick and choose which human lives you think are valuable or sacred. If you are against abortion, then you must be against capital punishment, you must be against euthanasia, you must be against systems of racial injustice, systems that perpetuate poverty, systems of discrimination, anything that threatens the dignity and value of all human life!

Pope Francis has said, "All Christians and people of good will are thus called today to struggle not only for abolition of the death penalty, whether it be legal or illegal and in all its forms, but also to improve prison conditions, out of respect for the human dignity of persons deprived of their liberty."

So, particularly on Good Friday, when we gather to recall the death of the Lord, his being tortured and executed, we should think of and pray for those who are being tortured and executed in our own day. In a special way, let us begin again in the hope of the resurrection to be Christian women and men who work to overturn injustice, who tell our civil leaders that it is not OK to kill, who stand up for dignity of all lives. Let's break away from any temptation to just feel sorry for ourselves, but instead repent and believe in the Gospel—recommitting ourselves to go out into the world and work for justice! And for God's sake, let's not forget the names of those who will be put to death on our behalf, for we in fact were and are there when they were crucified, and this should cause us to tremble, tremble, tremble.

IF THERE'S ONE THING I'VE LEARNED OVER the last few years, it is this: If you want to succeed, you need to learn to fail well. I first encountered this counterintuitive bit of wisdom in the lives of the saints, including St. Francis of Assisi, the founder of my order. But now, it is becoming part of the everyday wisdom of how to raise a child.

Recently I listened to a radio program on one of Boston's NPR stations in a segment titled, "Parents: Letting Your Kids Fail Will Make Their Lives Better." The basic premise was that many children, teenagers, and young adults today are crippled by the fear of failure, which arises from a number of factors and contributes to a number of problematic outcomes. Among some of the more immediate factors is the way parents are increasingly shielding or attempting to shield their children from any experience of failure. This might manifest itself in terms of large-scale overprotection, but it usually appears as parents interrupting the normal sequence of childhood and young-adult coping with the daily difficulties of life. Everything from a disappointing grade on a math test to a run-of-the-mill childhood fight between best friends elicits parental intervention.

The negative effects of this sort of interventionism and ostensible protection (recall that the "road to hell is paved with good intentions") range from an inflated sense of entitlement and specialness to crippling fear of the most mundane forms of daily disappointment in school, in one's career, and in personal relationships. If you've never failed, then how would you ever know how to negotiate the little and big failures, rejections, and difficulties you will inevitably face?

Some of the experts on the NPR program, including Hara Estroff Marano, an editor at *Psychology Today*; Jessica Lahey, a teacher and journalist; and Richard Weissbourd, a lecturer at Harvard's graduate school in education, expressed serious concerns along these lines about young adults at various levels of their development and discussed some of the implications for a generation coming of age with these sorts of hang-ups. One of the most resonating narratives came from Lahey, who also wrote in the *Atlantic* about the effects of this sort of parenting:

> The stories teachers exchange these days reveal a whole new level of overprotectiveness: parents who raise their children in a state of helplessness and powerlessness, children destined to an anxious adulthood, lacking the emotional resources they will need to cope with inevitable setback and failure.[1]

Now, I come from a family of teachers. My mother first taught elementary school and now teaches high school English. My brother taught high school before becoming an instructor in math at the college level. Both my aunt and uncle are elementary school teachers in New York. An important circle of my friends also are teachers: one of my best friends from college is a rock-star elementary school teacher in her district, another friend's wife teaches high school, another friend teaches high school in one of the most difficult inner-city districts in the US, one of my college roommates completed his PhD in education at Cornell, and all of my colleagues in doctoral studies are preparing for some sort of education-related career. My world is very much a world of education.

I've heard more anecdotal evidence over the years to support Lahey's diagnosis than I have time to rehearse. The stories can be horrifying, not just because parents, especially at the elementary and high school level, can be so rude, demanding, and accusatory with teachers who really only want the best for the kids, but because in the process one knows—especially the teachers who spend six to eight hours a day, five days a week, most of the year, with these kids—how destructive and unhelpful it is by way of life-skill development and self-confidence building to protect kids from failure.

I've also had, since 2009, the great joy, privilege, and challenge of teaching at the college level. I've had my fair share of the effects of this protection from failure playing out with interventionist parenting (which I do not indulge, stating to parents who call or e-mail that it is against

---

1. Jessica Lahey, "Why Parents Need to Let Their Children Fail: A New Study Explores What Happens to Students Who Aren't Allowed to Suffer Through Setbacks," *The Atlantic*, January 29, 2013.

the law for me to talk about an eighteen-year-old-plus student's academic performance, which it is, thanks to FERPA, and always direct them to the academic vice president's office if they have a concern). But that has actually been quite rare in my experience. More often than not, it is the students themselves who exhibit the anxiety, fear, and paralyzing effects of the possibility that they'll get it wrong. I even know quite a few adults and graduate students who also have these same concerns. Maybe you're one of them.

All of this is to say that there is a real problem in our contemporary education and parenting culture that has dangerous psychological and emotional consequences for a large number of people. One of the things that suffers most is creativity. It's not so much that an inability to cope with the disproportionate anxiety from fear of failure can make someone unintelligent or stupid, it's that it makes them uncreative because they can never take the risk that comes with creativity.

Surely, if you want to be a successful painter, you will at first fail on numerous canvases. And if you want to be a successful mathematician, you will at first fail in solving the equations. If you want to be a successful writer, your manuscripts will be rejected endlessly until one of them isn't.

But there will never come a point when you stop failing, because that's what creativity is about. What works can only be known against the backdrop of what doesn't—and if you're too afraid to ever risk establishing that backdrop, personally and professionally, then you'll never know what success is like.

There is a very Christian dimension to all of this, by the way. The Hebrew Scriptures and the New Testament are replete with failures—the disciples' constant misunderstandings, Peter's denials, the struggles Paul encounters with early Christian communities—not to mention Jesus's crucifixion, which we recognize and celebrate as something that is the greatest scandal and foolishness precisely because it is an objective failure. In the Hebrew Bible, we have the beautiful images in Jeremiah, for example, in the potter's house where he comes to understand that even as Israel screws everything up over and over again, God—like a potter with clay in hand—is patient and allows the remodeling to take place, allows us to try again, to become the beautiful creation intended from the beginning.

If we cannot live because we fear failure, then we cannot be good Christians because it is a faith predicated on being often diametrically opposed to worldly success. And as I say, I've learned that, just as in the educational, social, and professional world, if you want to be successful, you need to learn to fail well.

PRAYER, FASTING, AND ALMSGIVING—THIS Lenten trinity of practices has long been the foundation of our penitential season as we prepare for Holy Week and Easter. Many people will adopt new methods of prayer, engage in the spiritual practice of fasting, and offer time and resources in the form of almsgiving. Each of these helps us to focus our attention on what we might otherwise overlook and challenges us to, as one option for the distribution of ashes puts it, "repent and believe in the Gospel" in increasingly attentive ways.

Even when Lent is underway, some people might still be looking for a way to connect better to their faith beyond the usual tradition of giving something up. This is why I sometimes suggest that we might benefit from focusing our attention on something totally different, something often taken for granted: water.

With the short phrase "I am thirsty" (John 19:28) counted among the traditional seven last words of Jesus from the cross and proclaimed in the Passion account on Good Friday, it seems that we already have a reason to reconsider water as part of our Lenten practice of repenting and believing in the Gospel.

Too often this phrase has become overly spiritualized. It is perhaps too easy, too quick and neat to read this line symbolically as a reference to the waters of eternal life. There is a temptation here for us to ignore the real and powerful human suffering that comes with someone dying of dehydration and experiencing real, life-ending thirst. To overspiritualize the Gospel and overlook the real suffering of human beings is a problem because the waters of eternal life mean little for those who die waiting for the waters of basic earthly life.

In his book *Seven Last Words*, Fr. Timothy Radcliffe, OP, the former master general of the Dominican Order, makes the keen observation that, "because our bodies are 98 percent water," we might better view "dehydration [as] the seeping away of our very being, our substance. We feel that we ourselves are evaporating."[1] To die because of lack of water is perhaps one of the most dehumanizing ways for a life to end. And yet, millions of people face this threat every day.

Often, people in the United States are shielded from the harsh truth that most of the world's population does not have access to clean drinking water. This same insulated population, especially those in city and suburban locations, even regularly uses clean water to flush toilets, wash cars, clean sidewalks, and water lawns. That said, the recent droughts in California, Colorado, and Arizona, as well as catastrophes such as the Elk River chemical spill in West Virginia in 2014 that left more than three hundred thousand residents without drinkable water, or the tragedy in Flint, Michigan, have made more people in this country aware of how precarious life can be without the guarantee of clean water.

Beyond our borders, the situation is much worse. While we regularly accept the commodification of water contained in plastic bottles purchased at grocery stores or the use of filtration systems to enhance the taste of our already potable supply, the business of water has become a justice issue for those who cannot afford to satiate the whetted appetites businesspeople have for profit. It raises the question: Is clean water a basic human right or a product for sale?

Fordham University theologian Christiana Peppard engages this question in her book *Just Water: Theology, Ethics, and the Global Water Crisis*. Treated as the overlooked subject of Christian ethics and social justice, water, Peppard notes, is really a right-to-life issue, because "fresh water is interwoven with the most pressing realities that populations and regions will face in the twenty-first century, from agriculture to climate change to political stability, and more."[2] When we take clean water for granted, both humanity and the rest of creation suffer.

Jesus's cry of "I am thirsty" continues to be echoed in the lives of those hanging on the crosses of poverty and oppression. This Lent (or any Lent!), perhaps we can commit to rethinking the role of water in our lives, paying

1. Timothy Radcliffe, *Seven Last Words* (New York: Burns & Oates, 2004), 53.
2. Christiana Peppard, *Just Water: Theology, Ethics, and the Global Water Crisis* (Maryknoll, NY: Orbis, 2014), 67.

special attention to how we use and abuse it. In turn, we might reconsider our practices and discover ways we can become better sisters and brothers to one another and the planet.

ON NOVEMBER 10, 1958, THOMAS Merton wrote a letter to Pope John XXIII in which the famous American monk shared with the new pope some reflections about the world and Church. In one part, Merton describes how he has begun to understand that being a cloistered monk does not necessarily mean withdrawing from the world in an absolute sort of way. Instead, he has discerned the Spirit calling him to another form of ministry from within the walls of the monastery by writing letters, connecting with women and men that he might never have had the opportunity to meet otherwise.

> It is not enough for me to think of the apostolic value of prayer and penance; I also have to think in terms of a contemplative grasp of the political, intellectual, artistic, and social movements of this world—by which I mean a sympathy for the honest aspirations of so many intellectuals everywhere in the world and the terrible prob-lems they have to face. I have had the experience of seeing that this kind of understanding and friendly sympathy, on the part of a monk who really understands them, has produced striking effects among artists, writers, publishers, poets, etc., who have become my friends without my having to leave the cloister.... In short, with the approval of my superiors, I have exercised an apostolate—small and limited though it be—within a circle of intellectuals from other parts of the world; and it has been quite simply an apostolate of friendship.[1]

Merton came to realize that part of his religious vocation involved connecting with people of different backgrounds, experiences, and worldviews.

He corresponded with the writers Boris Pasternak, Czesław Miłosz, Ernesto Cardenal, and Evelyn Waugh; with activists Joan Baez, Daniel and Philip Berrigan; with theologians Paul Tillich, Karl Rahner, Abraham

---

1. Thomas Merton, "Letter to Pope John XXIII" (November 10, 1958), in *The Hidden Ground of Love: Letters*, ed. William H. Shannon (New York: Farrar, Straus, Giroux, 1985), 482.

Heschel, and Rosemary Radford Reuther; with bishops, nuns, and religious leaders of other traditions, like Thich Nhat Hanh; and with so many others including ordinary, unknown people.

I thought of Merton and his "apostolate of friendship" a couple years ago while sitting at a pub one evening in England. I was in the company of a diverse collection of people: a middle-aged father from Ireland, an Episcopalian priest from Scotland, and a woman and man from England, both teachers. We were there enjoying some beer after a long but inspiring day of academic presentations and workshops on the life, thought, and legacy of this American monk. We were in Oakham in central Britain for the Thomas Merton Society of Great Britain and Ireland conference, an event held every other year. (On each alternating year, the International Thomas Merton Society holds a large conference somewhere in North America.) I was there to deliver a keynote address, but the conference draws a diverse group composed of top Merton scholars, those with a more casual interest in Merton, and all sorts of people in between.

Strangers before this evening, those with whom I found myself at the pub all began to exchange stories about how each came to discover the writings of Merton and what had led them to attend this three-day event. Most shared a version of the typical Merton story, which begins with reading *The Seven Storey Mountain*. However, the Irish man recalled a dramatic event that took place in a hospital room. Visiting his father, who was recovering from surgery, he was told that the man in the next bed was dying. The dying man happened to be reading a book, which led my new Irish friend to reflect: "If he's dying and is reading, it must be an amazing book! I need to know what it is."

The book was Merton's *The Seven Storey Mountain*.

Decades later, this Irish man shared that Merton remained a major influence in his life ever since he read the book after that hospital encounter. Few writers and thinkers have such an ability to bring people together. Even fewer long after their death.

In 1958, it was Merton who wrote to the pope, but in 2015 it was Pope Francis who would hold up Merton as an exemplar of Christian living during his historic address to the United States Congress. In part, it was

Merton's reaching out to engage in friendship with so many people that led Pope Francis to the monk who had died nearly a half century earlier. Pope Francis told Congress and the world, "Merton was above all a man of prayer, a thinker who challenged the certitudes of his time and opened new horizons for souls and for the Church. He was also a man of dialogue, a promoter of peace between peoples and religions."[2] Pope Francis also held Merton up as a model for his own ministry, stating, "It is my duty to build bridges and to help all men and women, in any way possible, to do the same."

Thomas Merton continues to exercise an "apostolate of friendship," bringing people together across many divides. If you haven't met Merton and his friends yet, I encourage you to do so.

2. Pope Francis, "Visit to the Joint Session of the United States Congress Address of the Holy Father," United States Capitol, Washington, DC, September 24, 2015, https://w2.vatican.va/content/francesco/en/speeches/2015/september/documents/papa-francesco_20150924_usa-us-congress.html.

Having grown up in Central New York State, not far from the Adirondack Park, I have always had a special place in my heart for the beauty of deciduous forests. The green trees and shrubs, the rolling hills and glacial valleys, the clear blue lakes and streams illustrate for me the truth of Gerard Manley Hopkins's poetic vision, inspired as it was by the Franciscan John Duns Scotus, that "the world is charged with the grandeur of God."

That a Franciscan friar might want to write in praise of the beauties of creation seems like a bad joke or the result of a tired cliché.

Despite the apparent predictability of a Franciscan's sentimental attachment to creation, there is something that touches me more deeply than the immediately recognizable beauty of the earth. When I am awestruck at the sunset over an Adirondack lake or turn the corner on a road that reveals a landscape that takes my breath away, I reflect on the place we humans have in this world. This is in part because the landscape of upstate has shaped my theological imagination as much as it has informed my aesthetic preferences.

Pope Francis's commitments in this area may be original for the papacy, but for a long time now, theologians, pastoral ministers, and environmental activists alike have decried the ways in which we have treated and continue to treat the earth. We are well aware of the effects of our hubris resulting in global climate change and pollution. We know that we have a responsibility to the earth and the rest of the created order, and this has developed beyond older interpretations of Scripture that justified a dominion approach to creation that advocated human sovereignty over land and animal. We have come to recognize that we are not lords of the earth, but stewards of creation. But I have long wondered if even that is correct.

I am not alone in my incredulity about the popular stewardship tropes used, admittedly with good intentions, to talk about our relationship to the earth and the rest of its inhabitants. One well-known critic of this paradigm is theologian Elizabeth Johnson, CSJ. In Professor Johnson's book *Ask the Beasts: Darwin and the God of Love*, she calls for a renewed look at the biblical, theological, and scientific traditions that inform our understanding of ourselves and the rest of creation. She, like theologians Ilia Delio, OSF, and John Haught, reads the work of Charles Darwin not as threatening to Christianity, but as a resource for theology and our effort to engage in faith that seeks understanding. The result is a call for humanity to remember what has too often been forgotten: We are part of creation, not over and against it, not above or radically distant from it as earlier conceptions of an anthropocentric universe have suggested.

It is this insight that unsettles the standard stewardship approaches to creation. Rather than think about the whole of nonhuman creation as entrusted to us, which makes us cosmic landlords or property managers for God, we should consider our inherent kinship with the rest of creation.

Yes, we are called to care for creation, but that care shouldn't arise from some extrinsic obligation. Rather, our care for creation should be grounded in our piety. The Latin *pietas* means "duty" or "care for one's family," and stems from a deep relational connection. The care we have for our children, parents, and siblings should model how we think about and care for creation. In this sense, Francis of Assisi had it correct from the start: Each aspect of creation is our brother and sister; we are part of the same family, the same community of creation. In this sense, those who don't live up to their creational family obligation are not very pious at all.

When I hike through the Adirondacks and find myself overwhelmed by the beauty of God's creation, I am grateful to be a part of this community. The rest of creation cares for you and me; it's our duty to care for it too. And that's not just some romantic birdbath talk; it's the meaning of being part of this extended family.

DYSTOPIAN FILMS BASED ON DYSTOPIAN books have been all the rage in recent years. Hits like *The Hunger Games* and the *Divergent* series have sparked interest in the darker side of futuristic imagination. Perhaps for this reason Lois Lowry's classic, *The Giver*, has finally been adapted for the big screen after twenty years. But *The Giver* is not actually about a dystopian world. It is, ironically, about a utopian paradise.

The film adaptation, released in 2014 under the same title, starring Meryl Streep and Jeff Bridges, may be one of the rare instances in which the visualization of a powerful story enhances the narrative, rather than disappoints the audience. It opens with a world of sameness, reason, order, "precision of language," and black and white. All difference, creativity, passion, and emotion have been removed from human existence. There is no violence, no dispute, no variation—and it seems to be the perfect society in action. And as far as any citizen knows, this is the way it always has been and ought to be.

This is true for everyone except a community elder known as the Receiver, whose responsibility it is to keep safe the memory of what the world was once like, the world of diversity, passion, creativity, emotion, and confusing greys and colors. The Receiver is occasionally consulted for advice by the other elders, who watch constantly over the community, make pronouncements from speakers above, establish laws, and decide which persons (especially the newborn and elderly) are "released," a euphemism for homicide. The Receiver, who is getting up in age, knows how things once were and therefore is aware of how things could be.

The story's protagonist is a young man named Jonas, played by Brenton Thwaites in the film, who is selected to be the next Receiver. His responsibility is to receive the collective memory from the old Receiver, who by virtue of his instructive role now becomes the Giver. Over time, the Giver passes this memory to Jonas, who then begins to see color and nuance, to know suffering and happiness, to appreciate that things have been and could be another way.

Lowry's story is very creative, but the allegory isn't quite original.

It goes back at least to St. Augustine, from whose commentaries on Genesis we get a depiction of paradise, a prelapsarian world in which human beings don't act according to emotion, don't experience passion, and don't disobey the Creator so as to live in perfect freedom (*libertas*), by which Augustine means obedience to God's will as opposed to being governed by disordered desires, what Augustine calls "concupiscence." In paradise, human beings acted with complete rationality, which meant the absence of sexual desire and pleasure, as well as much of what we associate with everyday human emotions, including pain and happiness.

Augustine's vision of human life before the fall looks a lot like the world in which *The Giver* opens. The focus on rationality and absence of emotions suggests that harmony and concord once ruled, but that a single act of human disobedience—think apples and snakes—set everything on a dangerous trajectory.

This is the same trajectory the elders in *The Giver* wished to reverse in creating their own version of rational paradise. However, as Jonas sees both the potential for good and ill that arises from a complex and colorful world in which humanity exercises free will (*libero arbitrio*), he realizes that the risk of suffering and the messiness of life are necessary if one wishes to experience love and happiness, even if they are at times fleeting.

The Giver puts into stark relief an uncomfortable truth that human freedom comes at a cost, and the cost is the risk of abuse and misuse of that very same freedom. Some people, like Augustine and the elders, believe that the solution to suffering and pain is the elimination of choice and complexity. Perhaps some people, like Augustine and the elders, while well meaning, are wrong. If we all thought, spoke, and acted alike, things might be better—maybe even perfect. Things might be simpler, more black and white. Yet, they wouldn't be authentically human. The truth is we are all givers and receivers of memory, inheritors of the history of salvation that beckons us to exercise our freedom for the common good. Paradise isn't found in restricting freedom and suppressing emotion, it is found in following in the footprints of the most human (and divine) of all, Jesus Christ.

AMONG THE MYRIAD SUBJECTS OF FIERCE debate and ostensible controversy that arose during the 2014 Synod on the Family and continue in its wake, one in particular captured my attention. The question was whether or not doctrine can change or develop. And the answer, in brief, is that doctrine absolutely does develop. It always has.

One of the 2014 synod participants, Cardinal Reinhard Marx, archbishop of Munich and Freising, spoke publicly toward the end of the synod stating that Church doctrine "doesn't depend on the spirit of time but can develop over time." He added, "The core of the Catholic church remains the Gospel, but have we discovered everything?"[1]

Marx's question about discovery echoes his prelate predecessor Blessed John Henry Newman (d. 1890) who wrote the now-classic text *An Essay on the Development of Christian Doctrine*. Newman engaged this question about the possibility of change and development in the Church's teaching and affirms that both historically and theologically we must recognize that doctrine develops. Newman goes on to say that doctrinal developments were not only natural, but also intended by the Creator. Newman writes that many of the core Christian doctrines

> cannot be fully understood at once, but are more and more clearly expressed and taught the longer they last—having aspects many and bearings many, mutually connected and growing one out of another, and all parts of a whole, with a sympathy and correspondence keeping pace with the ever-changing necessities of the world, multiform, prolific, and ever resourceful.[2]

The central theme here is that though we may speak abstractly about a "deposit of faith" that is eternal and remains unchanging, we finite human beings do not understand the full meaning of these teachings at once. We

---

1. Eduardo Echevarria, "Development of Doctrine or Change in Teaching?" Catholic World Report, October 19, 2014.
2. John Henry Newman, An Essay on the Development of Christian Doctrine (Notre Dame, IN: University of Notre Dame Press, 1994), 56.

come to a fuller understanding of our faith with time, experience, and the guidance of the Holy Spirit. This was true going back to the pre–New Testament *kerygma* (early preaching of Apostles), through the earliest ecumenical councils (for example, it wasn't until 681 CE that the so-called Nicene Creed we profess today was completed at Constantinople), through Vatican II, and beyond.

The Church teachings on usury, slavery, and religious freedom are often invoked to illustrate the reality of development in Church teaching. But the truth is that there is a clear development—in Newman's sense of fuller understanding and clarification—of even the most fundamental dogmatic statements of our faith too. If there could be heated debates about the veracity of claiming the consubstantiality of the Son and Father on the path toward doctrinal definition during the first Christian centuries, then many of the allegedly nonnegotiable themes discussed at the recent synod are also fair game.

As Jesuit Father Thomas Reese recently wrote in the *National Catholic Reporter*, this way of thinking about doctrine in static, objective, and absolute terms is a return to what theologian Bernard Lonergan called the classicist approach to theology, which misunderstands the authentic development of doctrine and disregards historical consciousness. I believe that the reduction of Church teaching to propositional claims alone can be described as a sort of doctrinal Docetism—a misguided belief that faith claims simply appeared from above without any historical grounding. Just as the Christological heresy of the same name denied that Jesus Christ was truly human, asserting instead that he was only divine and appeared from heaven without any tie to creation, so too doctrinal Docetism is an outlook that denies the development of Christian doctrine as humans seek to understand their faith more fully. The truth is that God did not send us a preexisting book, a cosmic Catechism from heaven that states clearly and completely the unchanging deposit of faith. Just as sacred Scripture must be interpreted in order to understand its *sensus plenior*, so too sacred tradition must be interpreted and develop over time to understand its fuller meaning (see *Dei Verbum* 10).

It's important to remember that many of the early Council Fathers at

Nicaea, Ephesus, Chalcedon, and others entered the sessions over the centuries with views that would anachronistically be called heretical, only to come out with those same views ultimately declared as orthodox. We must trust in the Holy Spirit and be open to the possibility that we don't yet understand the fullness of our faith, and we have so much more to learn and discover.

EVERY YEAR WHEN LENT COMES AROUND, I find myself evaluating and reflecting, prayerfully considering my own ongoing conversion and return to God. But what does it mean to embrace honestly an examination of conscience at a time and in a world where racism, violence, and environmental degradation are so present?

Over the last few years, our attention has been drawn to events that reflect persistent realities of structures of inequity and injustice in our society. Because we are all interrelated in ways that are not always so easily recognized, few are willing to take responsibility for the abiding reality of social sin. It can be so satisfying and self-gratifying to assess our lives and actions by what we have done that we ignore the evangelical challenge to confess our responsibility for what we have failed to do.

That is why I believe that my prayer, penance, and almsgiving during Lent and throughout the year should begin with an examination of conscience, one that forces me to confront my own complicity in the structures that permit and perpetuate the particular sins we see on the news and witness in our communities. Here are just three examples that will be already familiar to anyone who follows the national headlines.

RACISM

The recent deaths of Michael Brown, Eric Garner, and twelve-year-old Tamir Rice at the hands of police officers have thrown our nation into a heated discussion about the treatment of men and women of color, especially by law enforcement. While the tragedies of lives ended prematurely are always particularly and uniquely painful, the persistent injustice of racism that provides the condition for gross inequality is all too common. Part of what permits its continuation is the denial of the existence of white privilege and supremacy in the United States. We must ask ourselves how we choose to view the world and whether we intentionally or inadvertently overlook how things really are. Those of us who are white (especially white men like me, who are beneficiaries of gender privilege too) need to recognize the unfair privileges from which we benefit in America. The benefits are often masked over by omission, by the lack of negative or oppressive experiences, by the absence of the skeptical gaze or the dismissive posture or the guilty-by-color association, by never having been targeted or judged because of the color of one's skin. Others don't have these privileges. Racism cannot be addressed until those of us who benefit from it, knowingly and unwittingly alike, acknowledge our privilege and own our responsibility to work toward surrendering it.

VIOLENCE

I have never shot or stabbed or seriously punched anyone. But still, I can recognize ways that I contribute to the prevailing culture of violence. Typically, unless we are direct victims of violence or know someone who has been, we are likely to go about living life as guilty bystanders. We are desensitized to the violence that is a daily reality for so many people around the world. We are often willfully ignorant of the physical, emotional, psychological, and sexual violence in our own communities. By not talking about violence, by not asking questions about human trafficking, by not thinking about what is happening beyond the comfortable borders of our own experience, we may still not be shooting or stabbing or punching another, but there is so much that we have nevertheless failed to do.

ENVIRONMENT

Pope Francis's incredible encyclical on care for creation, *Laudato Si*, has generated a lot of healthy discussion of the peril of our planet and our responsibilities. But still, in some circles the mere notion of climate change has led commentators to dismiss or negatively preempt whatever call to action and challenge to conscience the Holy Father has presented. It can be easy to be for the environment in word only, yet lack the moral fortitude and will to put that talk into action. How do I make decisions about what to buy, what to eat, where to go, how to travel, and how to live with the rest of creation in mind? What about the rest of the human family, particularly the poor who suffer disproportionately from climate change and pollution? We can advocate for changes in corporate and government policies that better protect our planet, but do we?

The purpose of this examination is to guide us in accepting responsibility for the particular ways we have failed to live out our baptismal vocation as followers of Christ. And these are just a few of the many aspects of our common life that call us to reflection; one could easily add sexism, poverty, homophobia, lack of care for the elderly, religious intolerance, or any of the many other systemic evils present in our world. So whether you are reading this during Lent or not, may we all spend some time evaluating not just what we have done, but what we continually fail to do. It's never too late to repent and be faithful to the Gospel.

Some of my Franciscan sisters and brothers will not like what I'm about to write here. And what I'm about to say can easily be misunderstood, so I will try my best to be clear: Contrary to popular belief, there is nothing particularly special about Franciscan spirituality!

I sometimes confess this perspective when I'm speaking to groups that have invited me to share insights about the Franciscan tradition, groups whom I imagine are eagerly anticipating the sell, the hook, the distinctive feature of Franciscan prayer and life. Often, these same groups at first appear disappointed when I share that, at its core, Franciscan spirituality isn't so very special.

The Jesuits have their Ignatian Exercises and Examen, the Benedictines have their structured life of *Ora et Labora*, the Trappists have their silence and contemplation, the Dominicans have their learned preaching, and so on, but what do the Franciscans really have? The Gospel. That is all.

This isn't to suggest that the members of the Society of Jesus or the Order of St. Benedict or the Order of Preachers do not have the Gospel; of course they do. But the Franciscan tradition advances only the Gospel in a way that is at the same time shockingly simple and incredibly difficult. Francis of Assisi begins his Rule or way of life for the Franciscan friars with the line: "The Rule and Life of the Lesser Brothers is this: to observe the Holy Gospel of Our Lord Jesus Christ." Sounds simple enough.

Francis goes on to say that the so-called First Order (the Franciscan friars) is to do this, "by living in obedience, without anything of one's own, and in chastity." But this mandate to live according to the pattern of the Gospel isn't unique to the friars. In fact, the respective Rules of each of the different branches of the Franciscan family begin similarly. The beginning and end of the way of life that Francis envisioned was just to live the Gospel.

This helps explain why there is absolutely no particular ministry or apostolate associated with the Franciscan charism. Nowhere in the Rule does Francis explain that it is the priority of those who would come after him to minister in hospitals or staff local parishes or serve as missionaries or lead retreats or teach at the great universities. All Francis says is that the friars are to work and receive in return "whatever is necessary for the bodily support of themselves and their brothers."

The vision that Francis had for his community was that the brothers would live together, pray together, support one another like a family, and work in the world among and alongside ordinary members of society. There was no special commission apart from what Christ tells all his followers to do in the Gospels. In other words, the core of Franciscan spirituality is the universal call to holiness that all women and men receive at baptism. In other words, to be a good Franciscan means to be a good Christian.

It is my experience that the simplicity of this message oftentimes seems just too difficult to accept. There is a temptation to complicate it, to qualify it, to repackage it, and to make it palatable. In its truest form, Franciscan spirituality cannot be reduced to any one thing or even a series of bullet points, which is why I believe that Franciscan spirituality is simultaneously attractive to so many people and also nearly impossible to articulate in terms of distinctiveness.

Pope Francis, who was of course the first Holy Father to take his name after the saint from Assisi, seems to exemplify the concurrent simplicity and challenge of Franciscan spirituality. That he is a Jesuit doesn't conflict with the Franciscan outlook because, as already stated, the core of this spirituality is the baptismal vocation. His gestures and statements are simple in the best sense. They are clear and direct reminders of the Gospel life. Whether preaching at daily Mass or connecting with strangers in an impromptu visit, he looks like a man trying to be open to all relationships in a way that reflects St. Francis's vision.

Though we may not all formally profess to follow Francis of Assisi's way of life, it seems to me that we can all cultivate Franciscan hearts open to what Pope Francis calls the Joy of the Gospel. This not-so-special spirituality is an invitation to a relationship with all people, to work with our brothers and sisters in everyday life, and to follow in the footprints of Christ. On second thought, maybe that is pretty special after all.

SINCE THE SENTENCING OF DZHOKHAR TSARNAEV to death at the end of the federal trial against him for his role in the Boston Marathon bombing of 2013, I have been thinking a lot about the *Catechism of the Catholic Church*. And I have been thinking that it needs to be updated.

After expressing my shock and disappointment at the jury's decision on social media—a response shared by the majority of the residents of Boston, according to an April 2015 *Boston Globe* poll, which showed that 66 percent of residents favored a life sentence—I was then appalled to see the negative reaction I received on account of my solidarity with Pope Francis, the US Catholic bishops, and even many of the marathon-bombing victims who were against the death penalty.

Amid the predictable nonsensical or tasteless remarks that populate the realm of social media, there were some more reasoned, if nonetheless still troubling, comments defending the jury's decision and the government's so-called right to kill a convicted terrorist. Most horrifying to me was the fact that several who espoused this perspective in favor of the death penalty pointed to the *Catechism* to justify their seemingly orthodox opinion. The least-nuanced views present the lack of absolute prohibition of the death penalty in the *Catechism* as somehow guaranteeing the right to pursue capital punishment. The more considered proponents argue that it's perfectly legitimate to support capital punishment, at least in the case of Tsarnaev.

However, neither argument takes into consideration the careful way in which the *Catechism* outlines, citing Pope John Paul II, the nearly inconceivable case in which the death penalty might be excusable. The *Catechism*, which is primarily a summary instruction manual of Church teaching for catechumens, states: "The traditional teaching of the Church does not exclude recourse to the death penalty, if this is the only possible way of effectively defending human lives against the unjust aggressor" (*CCC* 2267). This section continues, "Today, in fact, as a consequence of the possibilities which the state has for effectively preventing crime, by rendering one who has committed an offense incapable of doing harm—without definitely taking away from him the possibility of redeeming himself—the cases in which the execution of the offender is an absolute necessity 'are very rare, if not practically nonexistent.'"

The truth is that, in many places around the world, including the United States, there are effective means to protect citizens from "unjust aggressors" such as Tsarnaev. Secured in a supermax federal prison, an inmate sentenced to life without parole poses no actual threat, and therefore the death penalty is, according to Church teaching, completely off the table. Yet, those seeking vengeance and demanding retribution instead of restorative justice seem indefatigable in their clamoring for state-sanctioned killing, claiming justification in the *Catechism* because it leaves open the smallest possibility for a justifiable circumstance.

My proposal is that Church leaders give these people exactly what they want: a black-and-white answer to whether or not the death penalty is acceptable. The *Catechism* should be updated to clearly state, in light of the criteria already established, that capital punishment today is never justifiable. This would not only bring the *Catechism* more in line with the teaching of recent popes, including Pope Francis who has recently said, "The death penalty is an affront to the sanctity of life and to the dignity of the human person, it contradicts God's plan for humankind and society and God's merciful justice," but it would also bring the *Catechism* in line with itself.

The opening of the section of the *Catechism* discussing the death penalty reads: "Human life is sacred because from its beginning it involves the creative action of God and it remains forever in a special relationship with the Creator, who is its sole end" (*CCC* 2258). In the spirit of the seamless garment approach to Christian ethics popularized by the late Cardinal Joseph Bernadin, we must affirm that either all life is sacred or no life is sacred. For this reason, I propose also that the *Catechism* do away with the qualifier "innocent" when referring to human beings. While individuals may be guilty or innocent of a crime, all human life is without qualification; there is neither innocent nor guilty life.

Let's be clear. Those who commit heinous crimes deserve a just punishment, but the death penalty is anything but just. Given our circumstances, the *Catechism* should be updated to reflect the Catholic tradition's unequivocal defense of human life. Until then, we are still far from being pro-life.

Recently I had the privilege of giving a lecture titled "Vatican II and the Laity" at a parish on the Upper East Side of Manhattan. Those in attendance were wonderful, attentive, engaged, and lively in discussion afterward. One of the themes that came up in several different ways was the meaning of the shift from a preconciliar notion of the Church as unequal society to the Church as the people of God as presented in the constitutions and decrees of the Second Vatican Council. While the language of the conciliar texts, both theologically grounded and pastorally sensitive, was a vast improvement over the discursive approach to defining the Church prior to the council, there was a specter of Pope Pius X's "essentially unequal society" that continued to haunt the actual experience various people, especially women, had of the Church today.

Everyone could more or less trace the practical differences in the understanding of the laity's relationship to the Church by virtue of baptism and as the constitutive element of the Church, which is the body of Christ, prior to and after the council. Many of the folks at the lecture and those who participated in the discussion are liturgical ministers, theologians and other educators, leaders in their local communities, and so on. These sorts of opportunities were essentially unavailable or outright prohibited according to the preconciliar understanding of who or what constitutes the Church, as well as according to the pre-1983 Code of Canon Law (generally, the CIC of 1917).

Yet, many people felt that what Pope Pius X says in his 1906 text *Vehementer Nos* continues to prevail, if not officially then practically, in the ordinary experience of the laity.

> [The Church is an] essentially unequal society, that is, a society comprising two categories of person, the Pastors and the flock, those who occupy a rank in the different degrees of the hierarchy and the multitude of the faithful. So distinct are these categories that with the pastoral body only rests the necessary right and authority for promoting the end of the society and directing all its

members towards that end; the one duty of the multitude is to allow
themselves to be led, and, like a docile flock, to follow the Pastors.
(*Vehementer Nos*, 8)

One gentleman, while not explicitly coming to the defense of Pius X's turn-
of-the-last-century vision, suggested that in all organizations and facets of
life, there are necessarily those who make the decisions and those who, by
and large, follow.

I suppose that is true, and as the council documents aptly note, to talk
about the Church as the people of God and inclusive of all women and
men by virtue of baptism is not to suggest that everybody should or ought
to do the same thing. Just like not everybody should have the right to practice medicine or law, not everybody should have the right to every position
of ministry or leadership.

But what is to be made of the seemingly accidental (in the Aristotelian
sense of qualities verses substance or nature) distinctions that prohibit
certain members of the people of God, the body of Christ, from per se
participation in certain forms of leadership or participation in ministry?
This was a difficult discussion to have, but an honest and very good topic
still in need of further discussion.

This is particularly the case when the Second Vatican Council documents discuss the "vocation of the laity," attributing the vocational call
(*vocare*) to Christ alone and that all the faithful have a "right and duty" to
participate in the liturgy and in the life of the Church.

> Mother Church earnestly desires that all the faithful should be led to
> that fully conscious and active participation in liturgical celebrations
> which is demanded by the very nature of the liturgy. Such participa-
> tion by the Christian people as a "chosen race, a royal priesthood, a
> holy nation, God's own people" (1 Peter 2:9; cf. 2:4–5), is their right
> and duty by reason of their baptism. (*Sacrosanctum Concilium*, 14)

I made clear in my presentation that one of the most overlooked dimen-
sions of the council's teaching, especially concerning the liturgy, is that
the assembly is participating, is—quite literally—concelebrating with the
presider. So to suggest that everybody should necessarily be the presider or

lector or some other particular ministry within the assembly doesn't really hold if one believes in the teaching of the Church that the community gathered also makes Christ present (see *Sacrosanctum Concilium* 7).

Yet, the real question, and a difficult one to be sure, that continues to loom over all these great discussions is the matter of discernment.

As other conciliar texts, like the Decree on the Apostolate of the Laity (*Apostolicam Actuositatem*) and *Gaudium et Spes* make clear, the call or vocation of each member of the body of Christ, which is the Church, comes from Christ alone. How, then, do we understand who and how and for what Christ calls any individual person within the assembly of believers, from among the people of God? Furthermore, how is it that we understand the shift from Pius X's notion of "unequal society" to the renewed understanding of the Church that we have today? What does it mean to talk about an equal society? Can we or should we talk this way? What does that look like?

Considering these questions with an eye always on the universal dignity of our common baptism will allow us to see all women and men as equal in the sight of God, regardless of each person's particular vocation. Only then will we move closer to living what the Second Vatican Council has presented to us as our pattern of life in the Christian community.

Sainthood is a complicated and, at times, controversial subject. The significance of formally enrolling someone in the canon of saints is disputed, and the role of finances and ecclesiastical politics has cast, over the centuries, a shadow of incredulity over the proceedings. Coinciding with Pope Francis's first visit to the United States, questions surrounding the meaning and purpose of this sort of official recognition have surfaced in at least two instances. Both cases happened to center on North American Franciscans and, though they were centuries and coasts apart, both have attracted considerable interest and controversy.

On the West Coast, there was Father Junípero Serra, the eighteenth-century missionary sometimes called the "apostle to California." In the wake of Pope Francis's surprise announcement that he would canonize Serra during his September 2015 visit, some Native American groups have protested, accusing Serra of maltreating the native peoples he encountered in the 1700s.

On the East Coast, there was Father Mychal Judge, the New York City Fire Department chaplain (and friar of my province) who died on September 11, 2001, as he served first responders in a ministry of presence. Although personal support and veneration for Judge has continued to grow during the fifteen years since his death, some people remain uncomfortable with reports that Judge was a recovering alcoholic and may have been gay (though committed to his religious vows).

Are these friars saints? Should they be?

The situations are very different. In Serra's case, the concern is one of alleged wrongdoing committed against the native peoples of California, while Judge's case centers on the discomfort some people have with the complex humanity his story reveals.

Certainly, neither friar was perfect. But then again, that is not what it means to be a saint. Every saint was also a sinner, an imperfect and finite creature brought into existence by a loving God. Whether we are talking about Elizabeth Ann Seton and Francis of Assisi, or Serra and Judge, we are talking about people who responded—the best way they knew how—to God's call to live the Gospel and fulfill their baptismal vocation.

The *Catechism of the Catholic Church* explains: "By canonizing some of the faithful, i.e., by solemnly proclaiming that they practiced heroic virtue and lived in fidelity to God's grace, the Church recognizes the power of the Spirit of holiness within her and sustains the hope of believers by proposing the saints to them as models and intercessors" (*CCC* 828). This summary makes no mention of preclusive past mistakes or lives of absolute perfection. Nor does the practice of "heroic virtue" guarantee that each would-be saint never indulged in some vice in a moment of human weakness. To claim such a state would necessarily exclude everybody from the canon (maybe exempting Mary, the Mother of God).

Rather than resort to black-and-white thinking that paints Serra and Judge as either saints or sinners, perfect or imperfect, we need to readjust our perspective. Saints are to be held up as models of Christian living, as spiritual mentors and intercessors reminding us of our baptismal call. The catalog of official saints provides a rich diversity of Christian guides, and different saints appeal to different people. Serra has since been added to that roll, but what about Judge? Should he also be added? I don't know. But I do think that Judge provides a genuinely inspiring model of selfless Christian service. By all accounts, he was a friar who tirelessly served the people of God, including many of those few else would serve: the homeless, the victims of HIV and AIDS, the imprisoned, the addicted, the disabled. And he served those who risked their lives daily to help others, including firefighters, ultimately giving his own life in similar service.

It is a fact that both Serra and Judge were complex individuals that makes them so appealing to others and me. We should not whitewash Serra's relationship with native peoples, but acknowledge the truth that all saints are also deeply flawed persons. We should hold up Judge's heroic ministry, as well as call to mind his own struggle for sobriety. We should look to these deeply relatable Christians as models of God's grace working where we at times least expect it, rather than in the false perfection we desire in the saints of our imagination.

So I say, Junípero Serra and Mychal Judge, pray for us!

DURING POPE FRANCIS'S APOSTOLIC VISIT TO the United States in the fall of 2015, like so many who were glued to television coverage or who made the pilgrimage to glimpse him in person, I was captivated by the words and gestures, both large and small, that captured the attention and imagination of this nation and the whole world. From riding around in the visually humble Fiat to delivering poignant words addressed to Congress, it seemed like everything Pope Francis said or did was destined to be of historical importance.

And yet, despite the abundance of notable encounters, speeches, and actions that week, I found that I kept returning in my memory to an earlier image of him from the summer before.

The image is of Pope Francis having lunch. Yep, that's it. Just lunch.

Sitting at an ordinary table in what appeared to be a cafeteria like any one of the thousands located around the world, the Bishop of Rome sat in his white cassock amid uniform-clad employees of the Vatican pharmacy and facilities crew. And he ate his lunch.

That Pope Francis had lunch on July 25, 2014, is not what is really interesting to me. Nor is it that he chose to dine with employees of the Vatican. What is amazing was the way the world responded to this meal. Photographs provided to the Associated Press by the Vatican newspaper *L'Osservatore Romano* went viral on the Internet and appeared on the front pages of many of the world's most well-respected, international newspapers, including the *New York Times*. There was no major story accompanying the photograph, no peace-treaty brokered, no important speech delivered. It was just lunch. So what was the big deal?

It seems that the big deal was that popes—like presidents, prime ministers, and other world leaders—simply weren't supposed to be bothered with ordinary, everyday people. According to this logic, lunches with the pope were occasions reserved for important discussions of an ecclesiastical or international relations variety with power players who have their own entourages. That Pope Francis would elect to simply have lunch with just the entourage, the supporting cast, without any "important people" reflects the apparently unusual priorities of this Bishop of Rome. Nobody was vetted in advance; no political favors were necessary to get in.

However, such priorities would not seem strange to a certain first-century Jew from Nazareth. In fact, with the possible exception of an occasional physical miracle, most of Jesus's approximately three years of public ministry was spent without much fanfare or unusual behavior and with ordinary, everyday people. He spoke to them, even when others thought he shouldn't. He touched them, even when religious convention forbade it. He welcomed them, even when they were of another community or faith. He invited them to be his followers, even when there were smarter, more organized, and more loyal people out there. And Jesus had many lunches with them, the many anonymous people of no historical significance. Despite imaginations that suggest otherwise, most of Jesus's earthly life and ministry did not include grand gestures, fancy settings, or "important people."

There is an important lesson about Christian discipleship here. The Gospel is only ever lived out during the seemingly little things of the everyday. In office cubicles, on subway cars, along rural highways, at home or at play—in these places is where the quotidian reality of Christian life unfolds, or it doesn't, according to our choices. Too often we look to saints or other exemplars of Christian living and romanticize their famous actions or behaviors. We forget that Francis and Clare of Assisi, Ignatius Loyola, Catherine McAuley, and Dorothy Day all woke up each morning, went to bed each evening, and tried their best to follow Christ during the hours in between. What makes them models of Christian life is not some singular display of faithfulness, but instead the culmination of a lifelong effort to make the little things, like lunch or work, into moments of encountering others that then help proclaim the good news of God's love to the world.

Ever since that photo was published of the pope having lunch, and even more so since Pope Francis's visit to the US, I have been trying to imagine a world in which simple acts of humility, kindness, and concern for others was more commonplace. Perhaps then, such behavior, even by a pope, would not become front-page news.

PART II

....

Gospel and Culture: A Series of Short Reflections

I HAVE LONG BEEN CONVINCED THAT Christians, particularly Catholic Christians like me, do not pay close enough attention to the Word of God in sacred Scripture. This is especially true for those who are regular church-goers and those who have gone through the wringer of Sunday-school education or, as I have, received a lifetime of Catholic education. When we've heard the stories and know the characters as well as we do, it can be easy to overlook the manifold ways the Holy Spirit continues to speak to us through the Bible and recognize the ways Scripture continues to be relevant to our lives specifically and the world more broadly.

The aim of this section is to read the Bible with new eyes. I have included a series of reflections on passages that may be well known to many along with selections that could strike you as brand new. Whether you've read or heard the story before, it is my hope that you join me with an open mind and gracious heart to consider these passages anew. Perhaps you'll be surprised, just as I have been at times, at the ways in which the Spirit continues to challenge us as well as many of our presumptions about the world. Focusing on the moment, reconsidering how God's idea of justice differs from ours, exploring the ways we might find ourselves within the parables of Jesus today, and even examining the unexpected Christian qualities of a contemporary television host, are just some of the themes explored here.

Already, Not Yet:
The Eschatological Tension of Now
(Luke 21:25–28, 34–36)

Already, not yet!

This is a phrase often associated with the eschatological tension that is made front and center of the liturgical season of Advent. If Jesus is the "reason for the season" of Christmas, as the popular expression goes (though, in truth, God's love for creation is really the fuller reason for the season, that is the reason for the Incarnation), then "Now!" is the reason for the season of Advent.

Each Advent, as we kick off another liturgical year, it is worthwhile to step back and remind ourselves why it is that we celebrate Advent, what it is all about, and what it actually means for us (that is, "So what?"). As I am writing this, the readings for this Advent Sunday provide excellent insight into the answers to these questions.

The first reading from the book of the prophet Jeremiah (33:14–16) takes us back to the early centuries of the people of Israel. According to the Hebrew Bible (what Christians call the Old Testament), God makes four covenants, one each with Noah, Abraham, Moses, and David. The last of these is what is of interest to Jeremiah—and to us. The promise God makes is that there will be a restoration of the unified kingdom of Israel, which has at the time of Jeremiah's writing been split into two separate domains (not to mention the various capturing and recapturing of these from foreign nations). The covenant is that God will send someone from the Davidic line to restore the nation and community into one. While this is, on the one hand, about the historical reality of a divided nation, it is also, on the other hand, a prophecy that Christians believe exceeds the particular historical confines of the Davidic kingship.

God will, in fact, send an anointed one, a messiah from the Davidic line, who happens to be the eternal Word made flesh—God in God's very self! The unity that is brought about is a cosmic unity, not simply uniting historically separated kingdoms, but the whole universe and all people.

Jeremiah is not really aware of this in his time, but nevertheless expresses in his prophetic proclamation a sense of this eschatological tension between what has already happened and that which has not yet happened. The response is to address the question, "What do we do now?" and his answer is twofold: to remember the covenant, the past, in which God made this promise and to hope in the future for its fulfillment. Meanwhile, we are to live out this memory and hope in terms of working for justice in our societies.

The second reading (1 Thessalonians 3:12—4:2) likewise is concerned about the "already, not yet" theme of the season. The Thessalonians are deeply troubled about the length of time that it appears to be taking Jesus to return. They were expecting an imminent Second Coming, and what they got instead was a lot of anxiety about what would happen to those who might die before Jesus shows back up. Paul addresses this head-on in the spirit of Jeremiah, reassuring the Thessalonians by recalling the teaching and actions of Christ, placing their hopes in the future of God's promise and focusing on the present, the now. This is an admonition to this early Christian community to not get all worked up about God not operating according to their schedules, but instead focus on how one is to live in the now. Paul explains:

> May the Lord make you increase and abound in love for one another and for all, just as we abound in love for you. And may he so strengthen your hearts in holiness that you may be blameless before our God and Father.... Brothers and sisters, we ask and urge you in the Lord Jesus that, as you learned from us how you ought to live and to please God (as, in fact, you are doing), you should do so more and more. For you know what instructions we gave you through the Lord Jesus. (1 Thessalonians 3:12—4:2)

The season of actively waiting, of living into the "already, not yet" of our present reality is a season in which we should work to increase our love for one another and live in such a way as to reflect the Gospel that has been handed down to us.

If you're like me, then you've experienced the anxiety that comes with anticipating the future. We focus on what is to come, fear what we do not yet know, and remain uncertain about what lies ahead. Like the Thessalonians, we can be so paralyzed by the unknown ahead of us that we fail to see the world as it really is around us. Do we take the time to celebrate the joy and gift of life we've received? Do we recognize that God draws near to us, not only in the Eucharist and the Word, but also in the people all around us? Do we heed the wisdom of Paul and the instructions of Jesus that call us to trust in God, or do we only trust in ourselves? The season of Advent is a time that should shock us into such self-examination and reevaluation of our Christian commitment and how it is lived in the world.

The final reading for this particular First Sunday in Advent (we're in what we call "Year C" as I write this), is from Luke's Gospel (Luke 21:25–28, 34–36). We have within Jesus's extended foretelling of his death a promise of Christ's return and a presentation of what that might look like. The apocalyptic imagery that so often appears in Christian fiction or in movies about the end times that leads to fear and trepidation in the minds of many can mislead those who try sincerely to understand the meaning of Gospel life. And yet, Jesus's message here is really not about fear at all. Instead, there is clear instruction given about how to live in light of the "already, not yet" of God's eternal plan.

Jesus describes the end times (*eschaton*) with vivid imagery, but then offers a twofold admonition to his followers. He says that in the now we are to live in such a way as to avoid (1) drowsiness, drunkenness, and a sense of "taking life for granted," as well as (2) the unnecessary anxieties of daily life. With regard to the former, we can easily slip into complacency and forget about the Gospel call to live in the moment, to consider the example given to us in Christ. With regard to the latter, we can get so distracted by our own agendas, interests, and concerns that we also forget to live the Gospel. Both of these should be avoided.

What would it look like to live in the now? The question itself might sound a little tired or clichéd, but the truth is that to live in the now is to live the freedom of the children of God. Nearly all the saints we hold up as models of Christian living appear to us as fearless in the face of the moments of difficulty they encounter. I think of St. Maximilian Kolbe, the Franciscan friar who gave up his life in a Nazi concentration camp to spare the life of a young father. I think of Blessed Oscar Romero, the archbishop of San Salvador who spoke out against the violence and injustice of his society and was assassinated for speaking the truth of the Gospel, which unsettled those who sought only to increase their power. I think of St. Clare of Assisi, the cofounder of the Franciscan family who stood up to the pope in order to protect the way of life that she and St. Francis had founded on evangelical poverty. These and so many others lived their lives, day by day, in the now that exists in the eschatological tension of "already, not yet."

The season of Advent is a season of the now, it is a season that calls us to snap out of our quotidian malaise and our anxieties and fears in order to start living what we've been called to in baptism: Gospel life.

God Is Not Fair (in the Best Possible Way)
(Matthew 20:1–16; Luke 15:11–32)

I'm always struck by the zealous insistence of fairness as a rule that first appears in childhood when parents pronounce a decision that some child renders unjust: "That's not fair!" Growing up with three younger brothers, this experience was all too common throughout my early life. Sometimes it was an older brother like me who was given extra leeway, which upset the younger siblings who wanted the same freedom. Other times it was the younger brothers who were permitted to do something or stay up later than the older siblings were at that age, which seemed unfair in retrospect. In both cases, the feeling was one of personal slight.

Though this sort of protestation arrives on the scene during childhood, the socialization that led to this way of viewing the world surely began a very long time ago. Sometimes one is, in fact, not treated fairly and that is certainly an injustice. One only has to take a close look at the disturbing realities of racism, sexism, and the like to recognize the real unfairness in our societies. However, fairness as a rule tends to be more subjective than most of us would like to admit and it's almost always, at least when invoked by the comfortable or privileged, a cover for selfishness. We see this sort of cloaked selfishness in the way financially secure and socially privileged individuals and groups rail against political institutions that aid the poor and disabled, calling such necessary acts of solidarity and charity "handouts" in the most pejorative sense.

The Gospels are replete with illustrations that uncover our selfish impulses—those impulses that are so often and so easily masked by the ruse of fairness. Here is an example from the Gospel of Matthew (20:1–16) that does exactly this sort of thing.

You will perhaps recall the story, how Jesus announces, "The Kingdom of heaven is like a landowner who went out early in the morning to hire laborers for his vineyard. After agreeing with the laborers for the usual daily wage, he sent them into his vineyard" (Matthew 20:1–2). This fictive landowner, the usual stand-in for God, then goes out periodically throughout the day to hire more laborers. He orders that all the workers be paid the same wage, which provokes the ire of those who were first hired in the morning. This is how it goes:

> Now when the first came, they thought they would receive more; but each of them also received the usual daily wage. And when they received it, they grumbled against the landowner, saying, "These last worked only one hour, and you have made them equal to us who have borne the burden of the day and the scorching heat." (Matthew 20:10–12)

The fairness rule rears its ugly head in the contestation of the workers who labored all day. Surely, they insist, we deserve more than those who worked but a few hours.

But why? As Jesus's narration makes abundantly clear, the landowner has cheated absolutely nobody.

> Friend, I am doing you no wrong; did you not agree with me for the usual daily wage? Take what belongs to you and go; I choose to give to this last the same as I give to you. Am I not allowed to do what I choose with what belongs to me? Or are you envious because I am generous? (Matthew 20:13–15)

Or, consider another Gospel illustration, this time from Luke 15:11–32. One of the most famous parables of Jesus again reveals what's really at play in our own self-righteous thinking. This is, of course, the narrative of the Prodigal Son. After the younger child wishes his father dead and demands his inheritance, which he squanders, what would be fair is for that son to be dismissed and left for dead. Or in the best-case scenario, as the son himself imagines, he might be hired as a servant on his father's estate.

However, what happens in the Kingdom of God is the opposite of our base human impulses disguised as fairness. The gratuitous father is entirely unfair by worldly standards and welcomes the son back without punishment or shame. Like the vineyard workers who began early in the day in Matthew's narrative, the older son in Luke's parable seethes with anger at the spectacle of his father's blatant unfairness. Surely something he learned in childhood!

What is to be learned here? What does this say to us?

Let me suggest a few things. First, God's sense of what is fair and what is not fair does not, at all, align with our human sense of fairness, which again is typically a thin veil covering our own self-centeredness. The reign of God is marked by everybody having what is necessary. In both parables, God does not withhold anything from anyone. All parties are accounted for and given what is necessary for human flourishing. Yet, it is a sense of self-ishness and entitlement that drives those who have what is from the outset fair (an agreed-upon daily wage or all that already belongs to the father) to feel they deserve so much more. Perhaps this impulse goes all the way back to our mythical parents in Genesis, who were not content with their humanity and desired to have and be even more.

Second, these parables and an awareness of the selfishness that is called "fair" today spawns other narratives that then tend to justify real injustice in our world. The wealthy, comfortable, and powerful spin tales of fairness that are supposed to then accommodate their grandiosity in the shadow of poverty and injustice around them. Like the vineyard workers hired in the morning, many people seem to justify their greed and desire for more as a comparable reward for their hard work. But unlike the parables, the landowners and father (or mother) figures are usually not prodigal in their generosity and or love. Most landowners operate according to the logic of those first-hired workers. The rules then get set to benefit a few, while the system and the rhetoric of society explain inequality, abuse, poverty, and injustice as merely a real-world reflection of fairness.

It is difficult for us to accept the gratuitous love, generosity, and mercy of God. We hold one another accountable to rules of fairness, sometimes even baptized in the water of religion, but it is not the radical unfairness of God; it is not the radical justice that is equivalent to God's infinite mercy. I suggest that what our world desperately needs is a serious reconsideration of what we consider to be fair. (And hasn't the Jubilee Year of Mercy that Pope Francis instituted been a beautiful example of it?)

LOVE AND FEAR
(Mark 6:45–52)

FEAR ALWAYS SEEMS TO GET IN OUR WAY. Fear of vulnerability, fear of suffering, fear of appearing foolish, fear of rejection, and fear in all its forms govern our thoughts and actions when it comes to how we live. We create excuses, which are rooted in some form of fear, for why we can't love as Christ has loved us—we're too busy, too tired, too anxious, too unsure. We are, I suggest, most of all afraid of God's love and what it means in our lives.

This fear of love is, in a practical sense, a fear of God. And it is not new. Take, for instance, the story of Jesus's walking on water in Mark.

> When evening came, the boat was out on the sea, and he was alone on the land. When he saw that they were straining at the oars against an adverse wind, he came towards them early in the morning, walking on the sea. He intended to pass them by. But when they saw him walking on the sea, they thought it was a ghost and cried out; for they all saw him and were terrified. But immediately he spoke to them and said, "Take heart, it is I; do not be afraid." Then he got into the boat with them and the wind ceased. And they were utterly astounded. (Mark 6:47–51)

If Jesus's walking on water is an illustration of the divinity of Christ, then we have a not-so-subtle example of disciples literally fearing love, in this case, love that is God incarnate. What I mean is that if we take seriously what we read in 1 John 4:8 ("Whoever does not love does not know God, for God is love") and we profess that Jesus is God made flesh, then the fear of the disciples in this Gospel account is a subtle reflection of a fear of God.

Jesus's frequent refrain—"Do not be afraid"—should be our mantra of discipleship. Fear is what led Peter to deny being a follower of Jesus during the trial and crucifixion. Fear is what led the disciples to flee the scene of Jesus on the cross for fear of the same fate. And fear is what leads you and me away from remaining in the love that is God.

As the Gospel of John assures us: "There is no fear in love, but perfect love drives out fear." May we strive to love perfectly and, in so doing, remain in God.

(John 14:1–12)

EVEN JESUS'S EARLY DISCIPLES EXPERIENCED the temptation of turning what would become Christianity into a club. At various points, we read how some of the disciples argued among themselves about who was greater and jockeyed for the best position in the early Christian community. We also read in the Gospels how it was always the disciples, always the followers of Jesus who attempted to keep people away from Jesus. Whereas Jesus consistently welcomes children, the poor, sinners, and the ill, his followers seem to want to shield their Lord from the people who desperately press in to see, hear, and touch him.

There seems to be a perennial tendency to draw lines, categorize people, and label groups according to personal preferences and desires.

You are in.

You are out.

Simply because I say so.

Yet, to treat Christianity like an exclusive club for which one needs to associate with the right people or do the right thing to become a member is to misunderstand the vocation to follow Christ.

But Jesus intervenes to remind his followers that being a Christian is not about belonging to an organization or being a card-carrying member of anything. Being a Christian is about what we do and how we live. In the same chapter of John's Gospel where Jesus says, "I am the way, and the truth, and the life" (John 14:6) we also hear Jesus tell us, "The one who believes in me will also do the works that I do and, in fact, will do greater works than these" (John 14:12). The one who is the true follower of Christ is one who does the work that Jesus models for us by his life, preaching, healing, and loving.

This insight appears frequently elsewhere in the New Testament as well. What makes a son good is not what he says to his father, but what he does after the fact by working in the fields (Matthew 21:28–31). What makes a disciple loyal is not that she says "Lord, Lord" and professes faith with words, but that she does the will of God (Matthew 7:21). What makes someone holy isn't his well-planned life, but recognizing what is right and doing it (James 4:17).

To be Christian is to act in accord with the will of God after the example of Jesus Christ. Ultimately, one cannot determine for another whose side he or she is on. All God asks of us is that we recognize that following in the footprints of Jesus means recognizing the coming reign of God and doing something about it.

THE SIXTH BROTHER

(Luke 16:19–31)

HAVE YOU EVER BEEN PERSUADED to live differently because someone has been raised from the dead? The final line of Jesus's parable in Luke chapter 16 is one of the more striking, if overlooked, of his sayings recorded anywhere in the Gospels. Jesus anticipates the generations that will follow after his life, death, and resurrection, predicting that they too might not be persuaded to live in the model of his own life and ministry. Are you and I are counted among those generations? I think so!

Jesus says:

> There was a rich man who was dressed in purple and fine linen and who feasted sumptuously every day. And at his gate lay a poor man named Lazarus, covered with sores, who longed to satisfy his hunger with what fell from the rich man's table; even the dogs would come and lick his sores. The poor man died and was carried away by the angels to be with Abraham. The rich man also died and was buried. In Hades, where he was being tormented, he looked up and saw Abraham far away with Lazarus by his side. He called out, "Father Abraham, have mercy on me, and send Lazarus to dip the tip of his finger in water and cool my tongue; for I am in agony in these flames." But Abraham said, "Child, remember that during your life-time you received your good things, and Lazarus in like manner evil things; but now he is comforted here, and you are in agony. Besides all this, between you and us a great chasm has been fixed, so that those who might want to pass from here to you cannot do so, and no one can cross from there to us." He said, "Then, father, I beg you to send him to my father's house—for I have five brothers—that he may warn them, so that they will not also come into this place of torment." Abraham replied, "They have Moses and the prophets; they should listen to them." He said, "No, father Abraham; but if someone goes to them from the dead, they will repent." He said to

him, "If they do not listen to Moses and the prophets, neither will they be convinced even if someone rises from the dead."

My guess is that most people who hear this Gospel imagine themselves in the place of the rich man and reflect on how they have or have not cared for the neediest in our society. Yet, the instances when such poverty and human need are so starkly presented to most Americans in a way resembling the rich man and Lazarus are a rare occurrence. Far too often the rich and comfortable in modern society live blissfully ignorant lives in culs-de-sac or in gated communities a great distance from the poor and despised of the world.

Which is why I think we are more like the rich man's five brothers. From what we know of them, they are not overtly negligent of others' needs—unlike their now-deceased brother. Rather, they appear ignorant of what is expected of them, even though they've had the wisdom of the prophets and Moses to guide them all along.

We also have the wisdom of the prophets, Moses—and Jesus, who is risen—but does it matter? Do we live any differently? Or are we the sixth brother of the rich man, choosing ignorance over wisdom, comfort over justice, selfishness over solidarity?

In Giving We Receive

I LOVE THIS STORY FROM JOHN CHAPTER 6:

> The next day the crowd that had stayed on the other side of the sea saw that there had been only one boat there. They also saw that Jesus had not got into the boat with his disciples, but that his disciples had gone away alone. Then some boats from Tiberias came near the place where they had eaten the bread after the Lord had given thanks. So when the crowd saw that neither Jesus nor his disciples were there, they themselves got into the boats and went to Capernaum looking for Jesus.
>
> When they found him on the other side of the sea, they said to him, "Rabbi, when did you come here?" Jesus answered them, "Very truly, I tell you, you are looking for me, not because you saw signs, but because you ate your fill of the loaves. Do not work for the food that perishes, but for the food that endures for eternal life, which the Son of Man will give you. For it is on him that God the Father has set his seal." Then they said to him, "What must we do to perform the works of God?" Jesus answered them, "This is the work of God, that you believe in him whom he has sent." (John 6:22–29)

Similar to the crowd in Capernaum, we too can act more like we are interested in an immediate reward than as true believers. We'd like to believe that our faith is in something higher. Yet Jesus points out the embarrassing fact that, when it comes down to it, we actually focus on what's right before us: whatever will feed our bellies, grow our financial portfolios, or increase our immediate gratification. The temptation is to believe in whatever will satisfy us. But is that enough?

All the bread in the world and all the money in the banks would not satisfy our deepest longings. Like St. Augustine, our hearts will remain restless until they rest in God. But how we come to rest in God remains a little unclear.

So Jesus helps us to see more clearly. It's when we do God's work that our heart finds its true home. It's when we help feed the hunger of others, share our resources with those in need, and replace our selfishness for the self-lessness modeled by Jesus that we begin to recognize the true faith we seek.

It is no accident that Jesus connects God's work with faith in him. The way one best proclaims his or her faith is by good works, for actions really can speak louder than words.

To think of our own nourishment and satisfaction in terms of care for others and doing God's work reshapes our understanding of the most basic Christian prayer: the Our Father. To be given our daily bread, to be nour-ished by the Lord, is to recognize the daily opportunities to see the needs of others and respond.

Wrath Is Easy, But Mercy Is Divine
(Luke 6:36–38)

This Gospel passage is about as straightforward a message as one can read in all of the New Testament.

Jesus said to his disciples:

Be merciful, just as your Father is merciful.

Do not judge, and you will not be judged; do not condemn, and you will not be condemned. Forgive, and you will be forgiven; give, and it will be given to you. A good measure, pressed down, shaken together, running over, will be put into your lap; for the measure you give will be the measure you get back. (Luke 6:36–38)

It sets out a clear and direct message from the words of Jesus about how it is that we are called to be and act in this world. It also makes clear what God's priorities are and what God's actions look like. God cares for all creation, God loves all, God extends mercy to us even when we might think we (or others) do not deserve it. But that last part, that judgment we are so good at executing, that is a projection of our own human standards and desires, not God's.

There is a reading from the book of the prophet Daniel that is often read beside Luke 6 during the Church's liturgical year. It sets up well the human vision and practice against which Jesus is presenting the divine outlook:

Open shame, O Lord, falls on us, our kings, our officials, and our ancestors, because we have sinned against you. To the Lord our God belong mercy and forgiveness, for we have rebelled against him, and have not obeyed the voice of the Lord our God by following his laws, which he set before us by his servants the prophets. (Daniel 9:8–10)

Indeed, how shamefaced are we! We don't pay heed to the commands of God ("Love your enemy," "forgive those who persecute you," "turn the other cheek," "care for these the least among you," and so on and so on).

This is something I struggle with on at least a daily basis. Despite the years of studying theology and Scripture, living religious life in community, and celebrating the sacraments as a Catholic priest, I find myself wanting to return insult with insult, injury with injury, and hold grudges both large and small. It can be easy to think about the Gospel in the abstract, but it is very difficult to live it in the particular.

When we act with the interest of human priorities, skewed as they are by our selfish bias and hubris, we ignore the law of God and the consistent reminder to repent and follow that law exhorted by God's servants, the prophets. We sit on our individual judgment thrones and evaluate those around us and ourselves, promulgating judgment and declaring guilt. We say, "This is fair," or, "I deserve this," in a manner that all too often drowns out the message of the Scriptures that turns that self-centered logic on its head.

The life, the words, the actions, the death, and resurrection of Jesus Christ all reveal to us the way in which God wishes us to act in this life. If Christ is as fully human as he is divine, then we must recognize that his way is precisely what our way is intended to be. But we are so focused on ourselves that we cannot bear to consider it.

St. Augustine and St. Bonaventure describe the persistence of human sin as like being bent over, only able to stare at ourselves and unable to stand upright before our Creator and each other to see the world as it really is. Athanasius says that we have lost the ability to recognize or know God because we have become so fascinated and preoccupied with the lesser and passing things of our immediate reality. Far too many of us have become Narcissus, to recall the Greek myth, unable to look away from the reflection of ourselves or look toward anything that doesn't immediately concern us.

It is often for this reason that mercy is not our path; wrath is. Generosity is not our disposition; selfishness is. Forgiveness is not found in our attitude; anger is.

These things are easy and seemingly natural, they arise from our being concerned with keeping ourselves first and center. But Christ calls us to do something else, something far more difficult than minding our own business and watching our own backs. It is to love, forgive, heal, and be merciful in the way that God is already with us, even if we are so preoccupied with ourselves that we cannot recognize it.

When Prayer Becomes about Us
(Luke 18:9–14)

THE SCRIPTURE SCHOLAR LUKE TIMOTHY Johnson makes a very telling comment about this Gospel passage which centers on the parable of the self-righteous Pharisee and the tax collector (Luke 18:9–14), when he says: "For Luke, prayer is faith in action. Prayer is not an optional exercise in piety, carried out to demonstrate one's relationship with God. It is that relationship with God."[1]

This is a striking parable, one that gets me every time. It challenges its hearers to examine themselves in such a way as to confront with honesty the truth that (1) we are indeed all sinners and (2) that it is far too common a human trait to be like the Pharisee, to pray to God by looking out of the corner of our eyes and seeing those against whom we compare ourselves with despising or scorning glances and judgments.

How often do we find ourselves in the place of "those who were convinced of their own righteousness and despised/scorned everyone else?" My sense is that, if you're like me, more often than we'd like to admit: the judgment we may cast on our family members, neighbors, friends, or coworkers; the condescending remark we may make in response to a suggestion from another; the self-satisfaction that may come with a sense of personal or spiritual superiority when we compare ourselves with others.

In addition to the offensive self-righteousness of the Pharisee, we have other themes that also arise in subtle yet significant ways here. First, we must ask about the Pharisee—and, by proxy, about ourselves—according to what are others being judged as sinful, or "greedy, dishonest, adulterous" as the Pharisee in Jesus's parable puts it? The Pharisee (and many of us) appears to contradict himself in his prayer.

On the one hand, he's presuming God is a judge before whom he must make his case by highlighting the ways he is accordingly righteous. On the

---

1. Luke Timothy Johnson, *The Gospel of Luke*, Sacra Pagina Series, vol. 3 (Collegeville, MN: Liturgical, 1991), 274.

other hand, if God is the judge, then what business does the Pharisee have casting a verdict on the tax collector? See, Jesus does not deny that God is the judge, but as the Gospel that immediately precedes this one in Luke's account of the Good News presents to us—God's behavior as judge is far more generous and responsive than even the most surprising turn of generosity on the part of the so-called wicked judge who eventually hears the voiceless, recourseless widow and grants her justice.

The Pharisee wants God to be the sort of judge that fits his distorted worldview that is entirely self-serving. He wants God to render condemnatory judgment on those the Pharisee has already judged as sinful, wrong, despised, and so forth. But Jesus warns his hearers, using a passive construction in the Greek that signals it is indeed God's action and not the individual agents, that those who put themselves up like the Pharisee are in for a terrifying surprise.

Second, there is some truth about what the Pharisee presumes about the tax collector, at least that's how Jesus conveys it to us through the very words of contrition and shame found on the lips of the self-acknowledged sinner. "God, be merciful to me a sinner," he says. And he's right.

The odd thing here is that no one disputes—the Pharisee, the tax collector, Jesus—that the tax collector is a sinner. The only contentious question in this parable is whether or not anyone can stand before God and proclaim his or her righteousness. What makes what the Pharisee says wrong is that he too is a sinner, he too is in need of mercy, but his prayer becomes one of misplaced self-confidence, of certitude of goodness or righteousness on account of his relative social standing to the tax collector. But what might God have to say about this?

The Wisdom of Ben Sira helps flesh this out for us:

> The Lord is the judge,
>   and with him there is no partiality.
> He will not show partiality to the poor;
>   but he will listen to the prayer of one who is wronged.
> He will not ignore the supplication of the orphan,
>   or the widow when she pours out her complaint.

Do not the tears of the widow run down her cheek
  as she cries out against the one who causes them to fall?
One whose service is pleasing to the Lord will be accepted,
  and his prayer will reach to the clouds.
The prayer of the humble pierces the clouds,
  and it will not rest until it reaches its goal;
it will not desist until the Most High responds
  and does justice for the righteous, and executes judgment.
Indeed, the Lord will not delay. (Sirach 35:15–22)

In other words, God is not interested in a prosecutorial presentation of how great we are or why we are in need of answered prayers, admittance to heaven, or some other personal notion of salvation. No, God is interested in hearing "the one who serves God willingly," the one who is humble and honest and truthful about where he or she stands. And the truth is, as Pope Francis himself has reminded people in interviews again and again since his election in 2013, we are all sinners, we are all the tax collectors. But we so often act like the Pharisee, if not in our direct prayers to God, then at least in our thoughts and actions.

One of the overlooked aspects of this Gospel passage is the true meaning of prayer and how it can be so easily co-opted for selfish and harmful purposes, used to justify judgment and discrimination that is said to have come from God but really only comes from the minds and mouths of human beings, of other sinners. The Pharisee shows us how not to pray. He makes prayer about himself and not, as Jesus taught his disciples, about God's will being done.

Conversion, turning around, is what God calls us to do in prayer. To recognize, own, and confess to God "what we have done and what we have failed to do" so that we don't just stay in the place of our own imperfection and finitude, but move toward action and justice. Those who admit their sinfulness, who with Pope Francis identify themselves as sinners, are able to meet the other, to extend a hand of understanding, and to offer an embrace of solidarity. Unlike the Pharisee who has no need to be around such people, we are meant to be God's hands and feet and heart in our world to, as the Psalm says, "hear the cry of the poor" and respond to those in need.

> When the just cry for help, the LORD hears,
> and rescues them from all their troubles. (Psalm 34:17)

How does God rescue the just from their troubles? Through us.

But if we're too busy making our prayer only an argument to God about how good we are, how righteous we are, how much better we are than others, we won't be able to hear the cry of the poor, and we won't be able to be Christians. The time will come, then, when we will be humbled.

Jesus, John Oliver, and the Widow's Mite
(Mark 12:38–44)

WHEN I HEAR JESUS IN MARK chapter 12, I think about the comedian John Oliver. OK, I realize that that may sound strange, but allow me to explain.

The reason I think of John Oliver has to do with an episode of his television program *Last Week Tonight* that aired a year or so ago. Oliver and his team did a segment unveiling what began as critique of perceived abuse of the religious tax exemption provided by the Internal Revenue Service. It highlighted the personal wealth that certain televangelists accumulated while ostensibly fleecing their virtual congregants, many of whom were poor and even physically ill.

The clips of wealthy preachers calling viewers to donate their money to them in the name of God was indeed appalling, particularly in light of the stories shared by family members of deceased individuals who refused to seek medical treatment and instead sent what remained of their money to these charlatans. And throughout the piece, John Oliver, by way of his condemnation of this practice, seems awfully similar to Jesus in Mark 12, though perhaps Jesus does so with fewer jokes.

Too often, this passage (and its analogs elsewhere in the synoptic Gospels) have been misunderstood or at least misrepresented in a way that portrays a very different picture than the one I believe Jesus wants us to have. Typically, the observation of the widow's donation of her livelihood in the form of two measly mites (think pennies) is hailed as a sign of complete dedication and trust in the Lord. To be sure, this is the case; from this particular woman's perspective, we might imagine that that is exactly what she is thinking. As a result, preachers often claim that she serves as a model for us in how we should donate to the Church, giving completely from our livelihood and not merely from our abundance. We should give, they say, even when it hurts—just like the poor widow.

However, what is far too often not considered in this accounting of the narrative are the lines immediately preceding this observation of Jesus about the woman:

As he taught, he said, "Beware of the scribes, who like to walk around in long robes, and to be greeted with respect in the market-places, and to have the best seats in the synagogues and places of honor at banquets! They devour widows' houses and for the sake of appearance say long prayers. They will receive the greater condemnation." (Mark 12:38–40)

How quick we are to forget (or to project our own interests into the Gospel)!

The passage begins with Jesus's condemnation of the religious leaders who benefit from the convincing poor widows with lengthy prayers to pass over their livelihoods, their financial resources. In a way, we might imagine those who seek places of honor at banquets and want to be greeted with important titles to be like first-century televangelists (minus the TV of course). But when we read the passage in its entirety, we begin to see a bigger picture and recall that Jesus's mission is one of justice and peace, announcing the love and mercy of God in word and deed. His condemnation of the religious leaders of his time followed by the observation of this poor woman surrendering all of her resources to the Temple treasury should elicit a deep and troubling reflection. Instead of admiring the widow, we should ask ourselves two questions:

First, how did she come to be so destitute in the first place? Jesus notes that she's a poor widow and that two mites are all she has, at all, to offer. What are the social conditions and structures that allow for such a reality?

Second, why would she think that God wanted her to give up all that she had?

To the first question, we can look to first-century Mediterranean culture. Women had very little standing in the deeply patriarchal society. Widows, especially, along with orphans and poor children had little to no recourse and no legal standing. A poor widow is a person facing a dangerously precarious reality, whose very life is always on the brink of complete ruin.

To the second question, the answer is found implicitly in Jesus's condemnatory remarks. The sin of the scribes and other religious leaders at the time is the predatory practice of convincing the poor and disenfranchised that they needed to give what little subsistence money they had to the religious institutions in order to find favor with God. This is not something we can simply relegate to the past. It is a practice that exists today, something that is highlighted in the extreme by John Oliver's exposé of the predatory practices of televangelists. And yet, it happens in so many other ways, too.

To see how this happens in other ways, we need to think about the systems at work in our world that socialize people to operate against their own best interests. Oftentimes, the result is that a few wealthy and powerful people benefit while the most vulnerable suffer. For example, there is the still-contentious subject of health care in the United States. First, why do we live in a society that hasn't provided this fundamental element of basic human flourishing to all people? And why do those who go without health care support ideas and even politicians who want to ensure that this is not a universal right? Or what about the issue of income inequality, the gap between the haves and the have nots, the latter people which are encouraged to support and defend the haves as heroes without critical reflection on the reason that they themselves have not.

This Gospel passage is a call not for us to idealize a poor widow who finds herself giving everything she has to the religious establishment, but it is a challenge for us—like Jesus—to identify the scribes and others of our own time who are fleecing the poor and perpetuating the conditions of structural injustice, and then do something about it. Each of us has been given different gifts and skills that can be used in this work. However we proceed, we should proceed for the sake of justice in the name of God.

Come, Holy Spirit
(John 3:31–36)

THE REAL HERO OF JOHN CHAPTER 3 is the Holy Spirit.

Too often, the Holy Spirit plays the Trinitarian third wheel, overlooked and neglected in prayer and theological reflection. Yet, as we're reminded at least every Easter, we are called to be more aware of the presence of God sent into the world to draw near to us. This is a call that then orients us toward the approaching solemnity of Pentecost.

In Acts chapter 5, it is the Holy Spirit who guarantees the authenticity of the disciples' proclamation in the name of Christ.

> When they had brought them, they had them stand before the council. The high priest questioned them, saying, "We gave you strict orders not to teach in this name, yet here you have filled Jerusalem with your teaching and you are determined to bring this man's blood on us." But Peter and the apostles answered, "We must obey God rather than any human authority. The God of our ancestors raised up Jesus, whom you had killed by hanging him on a tree. God exalted him at his right hand as Leader and Savior that he might give repentance to Israel and forgiveness of sins. And we are witnesses to these things, and so is the Holy Spirit whom God has given to those who obey him."
>
> When they heard this, they were enraged and wanted to kill them.
> (Acts 5:27–33)

It is the God-given Spirit who enables the disciples to withstand opposition and overcome obstacles to ministering in the name of the Lord.

Though we don't live in first-century Palestine, we also are challenged to preach with authenticity, to be firm in the face of the opposition that will inevitably come with seeking Christ's justice, love, and forgiveness. It is the Spirit to whom we must turn.

Oftentimes in my own life, it is within the context of Christian ministry that I feel this tension between my own fears and the call from God to preach the Gospel. On more than one occasion during my ministry as a Franciscan priest, I've found myself challenged by the scripture of a given Sunday that speaks an unsettling word to women and men of faith. What is troubling is the way that I see the Spirit of God challenging our preconceptions—such as the permissibility of capital punishment or the widespread availability of firearms in our country—in light of the message of the Gospel. Sometimes, such as talking about the death penalty on Good Friday, the day Jesus himself was executed by the Roman State, it can be nerve-racking to accept the task at hand.

And yet, when I recall that it is not about me but about doing the will of God, not about my opinions but about applying the Scripture to our contemporary setting, not about my personal courage or talents or strength but about the Spirit's role in our lives, then I can do what I might otherwise prefer to avoid or ignore.

This, then, brings me back to John chapter 3, where the Gospel further endorses the gratuity of God's power and support through the Spirit. God "does not ration his gift of the Spirit," we are told. But with the gift comes responsibility: to proclaim the Gospel by word and deed. Sometimes the responsibility appears too hard. At these times, especially, may we pray for the courage to accept the gift and follow in the footprints of Christ.

The Surprising God of Easter

LIKE THE FIRST DISCIPLES DURING THE weeks and months after the resurrection some two thousand years ago, contemporary disciples (you and me) take time during the Easter season to look back with new eyes on the life, death, and resurrection of Jesus Christ. Or if we don't or we aren't, we really should!

John's Gospel is replete with resurrection surprises. Usually read on the Thursday of the fourth week of the season of Easter, this passage from John chapter 13 actually picks up where Holy Thursday left off. In it, Jesus serves as his own commentator on the events that unfolded just moments earlier, cluing the often slow-witted disciples into the meaning of everything he has done:

> Very truly, I tell you, servants are not greater than their master, nor are messengers greater than the one who sent them. If you know these things, you are blessed if you do them. I am not speaking of all of you; I know whom I have chosen. But it is to fulfill the scripture, "The one who ate my bread has lifted his heel against me." I tell you this now, before it occurs, so that when it does occur, you may believe that I am he. Very truly, I tell you, whoever receives one whom I send receives me; and whoever receives me receives him who sent me. (John 13:16–20)

If we think that all God wants from us is something akin to royal veneration, supplication, and distant respect, we need to reevaluate our image of God. John began his Gospel by saying: "No one has ever seen God. It is God the only Son, who is close to the Father's heart, who has made him known " (John 1:18). In other words, to understand what God is like requires nothing more than to look at the Son.

How Jesus loves, that is how God loves.

How Jesus forgives, that is how God forgives.

How Jesus serves, that is how God serves.

The God revealed most fully in Jesus Christ is a God who bends low, risks getting dirty, draws close to us, and cares for our basic needs—washing feet, providing meals, offering unconditional love.

The season of Easter provides us with a time to look back and recall what God is really like by calling to mind who Jesus Christ is and how he lived. It is for us, those who bear the name Christian, to then go and do likewise. I pray that I will.

THE PROPHETIC BURDEN
(MATTHEW 16:21–27)

JEREMIAH NEVER WANTED TO BE A prophet. That much he makes very clear. From the opening scene in the book that carries his name, this young man does his best—as do the prophets that came before and would come after him—to avoid the responsibility and call that God has placed before him. So by the time we get to Jeremiah 20:7–9, we encounter him in the middle of a serious lament. He is upset, which might be an understatement, that his preaching has led to personal ridicule, no one will take him seriously, and that those he has been sent to call out—those who abuse power and others, for example—want him gone. He's fearing for his safety and life, concerned that those who want to silence him will do precisely that. He feels in over his head, lost without direction, upset that his life had to take this turn.

And, in this moment, he blames God.

> O LORD, you have enticed me,
>   and I was enticed;
> you have overpowered me,
>   and you have prevailed.
> I have become a laughingstock all day long;
>   everyone mocks me. (Jeremiah 20:7)

Who else should shoulder the blame? It was, after all, God who insisted that the young would-be prophet didn't know better than God and that God had destined him for this mission from before he was born. Jeremiah feels betrayed by his creator.

But what should he expect? Those who bear the name "Christ" as Christians should be able to relate well to our predecessor Jeremiah.

In Matthew chapter 16, Jesus makes it abundantly clear that to follow him is no easy task. Jesus is not a sadist, nor is he encouraging masochism among his flock. Those who interpret the "denial" and the "taking up of crosses" as signs that Jesus wants nothing more from his followers than abject self-punishment are missing the point.

Rather, the denial of oneself refers to the situation that we, like Jeremiah before us, often face in our lives of faith. When the going gets tough, we'd rather get going back to our own plans with us as number one. We are hesitant or, more likely, completely unwilling to surrender the possibility that the world revolves around us and that we should first take care to be sure we're secure or comfortable or whatever before bothering to do God's will or help others. Instead, the denial has to do with our desire to place ourselves first. Placing God first instead shifts our outlook away from our own navels and out toward the rest of the world right in front of us.

In the end, like a good prophet, Jeremiah anticipates Jesus's message in the Gospel of Matthew. He understandably and rightly offers his cry of lament to God, embracing the suffering, fear, disappointment, and embarrassment that he experiences as a result of his carrying the cross of following God's will. But his exclamation doesn't stop there.

> If I say, "I will not mention him,
>   or speak any more in his name,"
> then within me there is something like a burning fire
>   shut up in my bones;
> I am weary with holding it in,
>   and I cannot. (Jeremiah 20:9)

He at first considers a plan of his own devising—yes, he'll stop doing what God desires, no longer risk preaching and proclaiming the Word of God. Instead he will be silent and enjoy the peace and comfort he once had.

Except, he can't do that. He realizes that he has a burning desire to proclaim God's Word, to announce the dissatisfaction that God has with the ways in which we human beings treat one another and the rest of creation. Though he tries to be silent, tries to enjoy a normal life, he grows "weary with holding it in" and must continue with the proclamation. This is what some Scripture commentators refer to as the "prophetic burden," the drive and fervor the prophet has to proclaim the Word of God.

May we find ourselves, even in the midst of frustration, embarrassment, discomfort, and doubt, with the Word of God burning like a fire in our hearts. May we grow weary of trying to keep that held in and, instead, dare to pick up our crosses, deny ourselves, and be the prophets the world so desperately needs. May we all share in the prophetic burden.

THE CHALLENGE OF (TRUE) CHRISTIAN HUMILITY
(Luke 14:1–14)

THE MESSAGE OF LUKE 14:1–14 can at first strike the hearer as lukewarm, especially after Jesus's rather dramatic and intense admonitions in the previous chapters of Luke's Gospel. Jesus tells his hearers a story about how to go about positioning themselves when invited to a wedding banquet. He says that one should not presume the place of honor, but rather take a lower place out of respect. To a certain extent, this sense of a lukewarm admonition is true. Scripture scholars affirm that Jesus's starting point is not entirely original, but rather relies upon the conventional wisdom of the time rooted in the ancient philosopher's proverbial insight. In a nutshell: Humility is a virtue (or, as I like to say, "Just don't be a jerk!").

So what is so special about Jesus's telling of this parable on the Sabbath in the presence of the chief Pharisee? Part of the specialness is elicited by what Jesus sees playing out before him in real time—various religious leaders are arriving at the location for dinner and are quibbling about who sits where and why. "When he noticed how the guests chose the places of honor, he told them a parable" (Luke 14:7).

The conventions of polite social and political behavior may have already dictated that people present themselves in a humble way, and therefore, Jesus's simple exhortation about humility at a wedding banquet (yeah, Jesus does not earn any bonus points for originality in cloaking his direct reference to those gathered in his presence at a Sabbath dinner) would be seen as a simple reminder of what to do when avoiding embarrassing social faux pas.

However, what makes this a parable is the way that Jesus takes what is generally understood and taken for granted and turns it upside down. It is parabolic because it bends the narrative line of expectation and turns it back on itself in a way that illuminates something new or otherwise unseen. Jesus is a master of unveiling, of prophetic discourse, of speaking the truth that others don't necessarily want to hear. So what is that truth?

I think it is twofold. First, there is an affirmation of the short-term goal of appropriate social conduct. This is a reiteration not only of the ancient philosophers, but of the Wisdom literature of the Hebrew Scriptures like we see in Sirach, which is often read in conjunction with the parable from John:

> My child, perform your tasks with humility;
>   then you will be loved by those whom God accepts.
> The greater you are, the more you must humble yourself;
>   so you will find favor in the sight of the Lord.
>   …
> Do not meddle in matters that are beyond you,
>   for more than you can understand has been shown you.
>   …
> The mind of the intelligent appreciates proverbs,
>   and an attentive ear is the desire of the wise.
> As water extinguishes a blazing fire,
>   so almsgiving atones for sin. (Sirach 3:17–18, 20, 28–29)

A modern translation of Ben Sira's wisdom in Sirach might be: "Know your role and be humble!" It is both a call to recognize one's place in relationship to others and a reminder to think first of what is favorable to God (whose view is far more important than that of one's social fellows).

So says Jesus to those in attendance, "For all who exalt themselves will be humbled, and those who humble themselves will be exalted" (Luke 14:11). There is something more expansive here than the usual wisdom. The typical social view was that one should avoid doing something potentially embarrassing and should take responsibility for this himself or herself. Jesus instead suggests that the ultimate humbling or exalting will take place from without—the implication being that this is from God.

As many commentators note, this helps us to understand the next ostensible non sequitur from Jesus to the host of the gathering:

> When you give a luncheon or a dinner, do not invite your friends or
>   your brothers or your relatives or rich neighbors, in case they may
>   invite you in return, and you would be repaid. But when you give a

banquet, invite the poor, the crippled, the lame, and the blind. And you will be blessed, because they cannot repay you, for you will be repaid at the resurrection of the righteous. (Luke 14:12–14)

Jesus's address here reminds me of the self-serving actions of those in power—political, media, social, and so on—on Wall Street or in Washington, DC, vying for more power and exercising that power in ways that, regardless of the superficial appearance, ultimately is deployed to serve the individual alone.

In a way, we might anachronistically look at the chief Pharisee with whom Jesus is speaking as one of these Washington players. Jesus's point is that humility for the sake of saving public face or personal gain is not the kind of humility that God desires, it is not true humility. John Martens, the scripture columnist for *America*, said it best when he wrote recently: "Humility will save you from embarrassment today and might even lead to a higher position at the banquet, but the exaltation Jesus is speaking of has to do with the Messianic banquet at the end of time—that is, places at table in the city of the living God."[1]

The honor that women and men seek in this world—demonstrated in the extreme case of Washington, DC, dynamics—is not the honor that is proper to right relationship with God and others. Martens further explains:

> True honor is found in humility, and true humility is located in seeking the needs of others, not one's own. Honor might never be gained in this world for seeking out the poor and the needy, and repayment might come only in the new age, when honor and shame, like poverty and wealth, are burned up in the glory of God. At the banquet in the city of God, all sit in positions of equal rank and all share in the grace that reveals us all to be members of God's one family.

In this way, Jesus is truly unsettling the hearers of the Word of God. These people would expect a popular preacher like Jesus to give them an earful of conventional wisdom, but instead takes their familiar worldviews and turns

---

1. John W. Martens, "The City of the Living God," *America* (August 26—September 2, 2013), 29.

them around to illustrate what God really desires: that we exhibit humility and refuse pretense when we do what ought to be done for those who need it the most without any expectation of return, including the short-term goal of avoiding embarrassment in a social setting.

Jesus says, "If you continue in my word, you are truly my disciples; and you will know the truth, and the truth will make you free" (John 8:31–32). But, as if fulfilling the prophecy of Jack Nicholson's character in *A Few Good Men*, those who hear Jesus seem quite incapable of handling the truth.

The question of Pilate lingers in the background of Jesus's curious line: *quid veritas est?* What is this truth about which Jesus is speaking, according to which one who would be his disciple would be set free? It seems that Jesus is both rather straightforward and curiously deceptive about what precisely he means.

To have a better sense of this idea of truth as it is used in this case, scholars, as usual, are divided on what exactly Jesus intends. The most plausible referent, however, is likely the revelation of God in the very person Jesus of Nazareth. His life, words, and deeds as exhibited throughout John's Gospel—otherwise described as the book of these signs—bespeak a truth that cannot be intuited from our own experience. Rather, the truth that sets the disciple free is the very word of Christ, which in Hebrew (*dabar*) denotes not just what one says, but action, event, and dynamism. In this sense, the opening of John's Gospel makes more sense than it ordinarily might to our Hellenistic ears: the Word became flesh. The Word acts.

Knowing the *dabar* of Jesus is to know the fullest revelation of God (see John 1:18, in which we are told at the end of the prologue that "no one has ever seen God. It is God the only Son…who has made him known"), which is both the content of the message and the transformative power of the action. And to know the truth that sets one free is to embrace the relationality of God's intention for all of us. Jesus tries to express this in his dialogue with, interestingly enough, "those who had believed in him," the group of people he is addressing in this passage. But like so many who today profess to believe in him or, as the PEW Research polls continually tell us, admit to having had professed belief in him, the audience of Jesus's time misses the point.

"Oh, I know what it means to follow the Law and to do what God instructed us through Abraham," they reply. But Jesus tries to get across that something entirely new is unfolding. What they take to be the instructions according to Abraham their father in faith is, Jesus seems to claim, actually their own misinterpretations and a straying away from what it is that God reveals to Abraham, Isaac, Jacob, and so on. He says, "If you were Abraham's children, you would be doing what Abraham did" (John 8:39). Instead, if even sincerely, they are doing the works of their own liking, not those revealed by God to their ancestors.

How true is that for Christians today? "We are disciples of Jesus and we do his works!" we might easily say. But how faithfully, how truly, do we really? I know that I fail all the time. I forget; I struggle too.

We who bear the name Christ and call ourselves Christian should do his works according to his Word (*dabar*), but so often we mistake our own social, cultural, and personal desires for the Word of God. This is how some self-identified Christians end up committing all sorts of hatred, discrimination, and violence. But this is also how more ordinary women and men like you and me, who also bear the name Christ, end up judging and excluding, seeking wealth, and ignoring the poor, advancing our own power while marginalizing those who already have no voice. This is not the truth about which Jesus speaks.

Jesus's truth, the truth of the Word of God, is a truth of radical relationship and self-sacrificial love (*agape*). It is a love of neighbor and stranger and enemy that is peace that the world cannot give, as Paul says, that is foolishness and stupidity to the world, but it is the heart of who God is and who we are called to be. It is a truth that can set us free by unveiling and then removing the strictures we place on ourselves and others in our self-serving actions and attitudes. It is a truth that is not so much easily understood as challengingly lived out.

Have You Met Simon's Mother-in-Law?
(Mark 1:29–31)

I USED TO DISLIKE THIS STORY ABOUT the healing of Simon's mother-in-law. There was something that struck my modern awareness of the subjugation of women in various times and cultures that suggested her immediate service or waiting on Jesus, Simon, Andrew, and the gang right after she was healed from her illness was offensive. That is, until I had a better appreciation for the connection between this passage, which appears in the first chapter of Mark's Gospel, and one that appears eight chapters later.

For starters, this is the first passage, including the bit that once made me uncomfortable:

> As soon as they left the synagogue, they entered the house of Simon and Andrew, with James and John. Now Simon's mother-in-law was in bed with a fever, and they told him about her at once. He came and took her by the hand and lifted her up. Then the fever left her, and she began to serve them. (Mark 1:29–31)

What is interesting is that what is really being described is Simon's (unfortunately unnamed) mother-in-law's *diakonos*. Her service or waiting on them is not simply the labor of someone confined to domestic servitude, doing the stereotypical woman's work of a subjugated first-century woman, but the action of a disciple following in the truest sense the example and call of Jesus Christ.

It is no accident that she does this immediately after receiving the healing touch of Jesus.

Having been healed of her illness, of her brokenness, of her separation from the life of community in seclusion, she recognizes—perhaps only intuitively, but certainly by the Spirit—that it falls to her to share that healing gift of service, *diakonos*, with others in return for God's love and healing.

This is the same language that is then used later in Mark when Jesus comes across his bickering disciples on a walk along the road. They fight over who is the greatest, and Jesus, drawing on the same action, the same *diakonos*, of Simon's mother-in-law, tells the two clueless followers that the greatest disciple is the one who does what Simon's mother-in-law does: Recognize the healing presence of God in his or her life and then serves others.

It is rather unexpected, I suppose, but a great model no less. Instead of a symbol of subjugation and marginalization, it turns out that the service (*diakonos*) of Simon's mother-in-law is a model of authentic and true Christian discipleship.

When Jesus Broke the Rules
(Mark 3:1–6)

WHAT DO YOU DO WHEN YOU KNOW what is right, but the rules forbid it?

This question lies at the center of a story when Jesus is, according to this account, somewhat entrapped by the Pharisees; they are apparently looking for any excuse to silence and get rid of him. The motive of the onlookers is made plain: "They watched him...so that they might accuse him" (Mark 3:2). The priorities of God in Jesus and priorities of those concerned with maintaining the status quo clearly surface:

> Again he entered the synagogue, and a man was there who had a withered hand. They watched him to see whether he would cure him on the sabbath, so that they might accuse him. And he said to the man who had the withered hand, "Come forward." Then he said to them, "Is it lawful to do good or to do harm on the sabbath, to save life or to kill?" But they were silent. He looked around at them with anger; he was grieved at their hardness of heart and said to the man, "Stretch out your hand." He stretched it out, and his hand was restored. The Pharisees went out and immediately conspired with the Herodians against him, how to destroy him. (Mark 3:1–6)

What is most interesting are the starting points of both Jesus and the onlooking Pharisees. It's easy to look at this scenario and, with the twenty-twenty hindsight of Mark's narrative, quickly castigate the Pharisees for their lack of sensitivity, their misguided prioritization of law over person, and the ostensible plotting that leads to their desire to entrap Jesus. However, these were religious leaders of the age trying to do what they thought was right. Given the benefit of the doubt, the Pharisees, in their concern for the proper observance of the Sabbath, were striving not to protect their own laws but those of God. For as any good Jew or Christian should intuitively know, the Decalogue (the Ten Commandments) contains this command from God to keep holy the Sabbath. These religious leaders likely thought that they were doing the right thing, that they were simply obeying the desire of God and exhorting others to do likewise.

It is also easy for us to look at the scenario and see that Jesus is the Word made flesh as we, in faith, proclaim, thereby anachronistically trumping the Pharisees' interpretation of the Torah. For who would know the law of God better than God?

But there is an uneasy conflict here. God, in Jesus Christ, is rejected no less for the actualization of God's law in the most authentic manner by those who at the same time strive, in the name of the same law, to protect that structure for living. The key—the condition for the very possibility of this rejection and conflict—arises in the subtle, unconscious, and even sincere misplacement of priorities. So often religious leaders and all people of faith can mistake the human interpretations of God's law, God's rules for authentic human living, for God's command itself. This happened and was called out by Jesus Christ in the first century, and it happens and is occasionally called out today.

Who someone is supposed to love, how someone is to relate to others, what sort of work or ministry someone is supposed to do, who can or cannot participate in what ways in the life of the faith community, and so on, these remain examples of human interpretations of God's law and desire even today.

So what does it mean when Jesus breaks the rules? Is this a clarion cry for all women and men of faith to engage in ecclesiastical disobedience? I don't think so. It's not a wild-card justification or a blank check to justify whatever view we wish to espouse or action we wish to pursue. When Jesus broke the rules as he did in today's Gospel, he did so to point out what God's priorities really are: Do good...save life. These must always take priority.

Marginalization, discrimination, violence, hatred, and so forth, even dressed up in the sheep's clothing of legal righteousness and religious zeal, are nevertheless indications that the priorities of God are being supplanted by the personal or collective interests of human beings. One only has to look to Jesus, the fullness of God's self-disclosure and the very exegesis of God, to find example after example of what divine priority really looks like.

When Jesus broke the rules, he did so for the sake of the other and never for his own personal gain. Nothing summarizes this truth better than the crosses we affix to walls and churches and chains around our necks. God does not care about our justifications for the unjust rules that some so passionately defend. God only desires that we do good and save life, even if it means breaking the rules.

I HAVE COME TO REALIZE THAT LUKE chapter 13 makes me uncomfortable, and that this is probably a good thing.

There are plenty of places in sacred scripture that are supposed to do that to us. For instance, consider Isaiah 66:18–21 and what the original hearers of this prophetic speech would have thought: "For I know their works and their thoughts, and I am coming to gather all nations and tongues.... They shall bring all your kindred from all the nations as an offering to the Lord" (Isaiah 66:18, 20).

The chosen people of God might have been unhappy to hear about how God's desire is for all nations to come together, that the people of God—a favored term of the Second Vatican Council fathers for the whole Church—extended far beyond that of the community of Israel. If one cannot be separate, apart, holy in the literal sense—then what makes one special?

Yet, this is God's desire and plan and vision of reality: All of God's creation, every human person is a son or daughter, and therefore a brother and sister to each other. There might be times when it is more difficult than others for us to appreciate this about individuals or groups of people that we have come to dislike for a variety of reasons, but God's wisdom insists that this is for us to overcome and that it is not God's intention that we be divided.

This is indeed a hard truth, just as much for us today in the United States as it was for the Israelites thousands of years earlier. The vilification of other people in other lands, the maintenance of prejudice and racial discrimination, our resistance to welcome the stranger into our midst, the perpetuation of inequality in pay and social standing for women, the continued prohibition of certain civil rights for all—these are just some of the ways in which we struggle as a nation against God's will for inclusivity and recognition of all people as equal in the sight of their Creator.

Or consider this passage from the Letter to the Hebrews (12:5–7, 11–13); it may set you on edge. It is quite understandable that it could, for the author makes it clear that being a disciple of Christ requires the acceptance of difficult or challenging times. And why shouldn't it? Didn't Jesus, the letter's author explains, endure the trials and demonstrate the discipline necessary to do what is right? Why should we, who call ourselves Christians and bear the name of Christ, expect anything different?

> Now, discipline always seems painful rather than pleasant at the time, but later it yields the peaceful fruit of righteousness to those who have been trained by it. (Hebrews 12:11)

All of which brings me round to the unsettling Gospel of Luke 13. Here, Jesus seems to do something that is commonplace in my experience of human nature and something that I'm sure frustrates a whole host of other people. He doesn't answer a straightforward question!

> Someone asked him, "Lord, will only a few be saved?" He said to them, "Strive to enter through the narrow door; for many, I tell you, will try to enter and will not be able." (Luke 13:23–24)

He does not outrightly answer the question posed to him. Some people might misread his response as an answer to the question. Likewise, some will interpret his saying that "many...will attempt" and claim that this indicates that only few will enter.

Yet, this is not exactly right. Jesus is redirecting the focus of the questioner and his other hearers (including us) away from what teachers often refer to as stupid questions. The curious (or perhaps cunning) person who posed the question basically asks the wrong question, so Jesus proceeds to respond the answer to the right question that was never asked!

Instead of being concerned with who is in and who is out, those who follow in the footprints of Christ should be concerned with rising to the challenges of discipleship we are sure to encounter throughout our lives. It is like looking at two ways to enter a location—one is wide and easy and filled with the mob of those unwilling or unable to embrace the cross of discipleship, and the other is narrow and more difficult. Jesus says that we should not focus simply on the ends (that is, who is in or out), but instead focus our attention on the means (that is, doing what is right even when it is difficult)!

This Jesus explains again in the second part of Luke's Gospel passage, when he presents an allegory that can also be uncomfortable to hear:

> When once the owner of the house has got up and shut the door, and you begin to stand outside and to knock at the door, saying, "Lord, open to us," then in reply he will say to you, "I do not know where you come from." Then you will begin to say, "We ate and drank with you, and you taught in our streets." But he will say, "I do not know where you come from; go away from me, all you evil-doers!" There will be weeping and gnashing of teeth when you see Abraham and Isaac and Jacob and all the prophets in the kingdom of God, and you yourselves thrown out. Then people will come from east and west, from north and south, and will eat in the kingdom of God. (Luke 13:25–29)

Those would-be disciples that are so concerned about who is in and who is out must realize, Jesus explains, that just because you claim to be a Christian, just because you associate with Jesus, just because you think you're in the in crowd, doesn't mean that you're going to make it.

Actions speak louder than words, and to be part of God's reign is demonstrated not by who you know, but how you live.

This is why Jesus can talk about all the people from, literally, all the ends of the earth that will "eat in the Kingdom of God," while those who were so sure of themselves and did little else will not. Those who think themselves the first in the line of Christian discipleship might experience a harsh awakening that they are indeed last in word and deed, while those who were written off because they didn't think, look, or behave a certain prescribed way according to the self-identified firsts in line will be reclining with Christ at the table.

PART III
Vowed Life Today

Too often the conversation within church circles about vowed life centers on people like me: someone in consecrated religious life. Priests, nuns, brothers—these are the women and men that typically first come to mind when we think about someone having a Christian vocation. And while it is certainly true and accurate to talk in this manner, such a narrow conception does not begin to touch the richness and depth of what it means to think of the Christian life of discipleship to which all the baptized are called.

This last section is dedicated to considering the ways we might reimagine both the meaning of consecrated religious life and other, equally dignified forms of Christian living in the contemporary world. Those who are single or married, work in business or service-based fields, live in cities or in rural settings—regardless of one's state in life, everybody that identifies as a Christian has received a call by virtue of baptism. This call is to follow in the footprints of Jesus Christ and live after the pattern of the Gospel. How one does this in his or her particular setting is really determined by a number of factors unique to each individual's social location. Nevertheless, there are persistent themes that transcend the stereotypical boundaries we have long maintained between one another.

These reflections are presented as an invitation to reimagine our lives of Christian discipleship and the meaning of vocation. Just as we all renew the vows of our baptism during the Easter season of the Church's liturgical year, these essays are presented as an opportunity to reflect on what it is we believe, how we are living, and what it means to reflect the life of the Gospel in our modern world.

IN THE BEGINNING WAS THE WORD, but who heard it?

The prologue to John's Gospel reminds us that though Christ entered our world as one of us, we who were in the world did not recognize him (John 1:9–13). So many did not hear him, so many would not hear him. Has anything really changed?

With declining church attendance and lower numbers of those entering the ministerial priesthood and religious life in many parts of the world, it can seem like nothing has changed.

But before despairing about a world deaf to the Word of God, I should say there is tremendous hope that not only should "all those who have ears ought to hear" (Matthew 13:9), but that many indeed do hear the Word, have hearts open to the Spirit, and live the call they have been given by God. Among these are women and men who have entered religious life and professed the evangelical counsels (poverty, chastity, and obedience).

Pope Francis recently had us spend a year celebrating consecrated religious life, coinciding with the church's celebration of the fiftieth anniversary of the Second Vatican Council. Whereas religious life was once mistaken for a superior way of being a Christian prior to Vatican II, the Council called religious communities to return to their original charism, focusing especially on the centrality of baptism in discipleship. The result has been a renewed sense of the meaning and purpose of consecrated life, not as something absolutely set apart from the rest of the faithful, but rather, as a particular iteration of a response to God's call. Therefore, consecrated life in today's world is one sign of what it means to hear the Word and live the call, a reminder to all that each person has a vocation.

Over the centuries, several Christian theologians, spiritual writers, and saints have helped the church to remember that every person has a vocation from God. For example, the German Jesuit theologian Karl Rahner, a key theological advisor at Vatican II, emphasized that every human being had the "capacity for God" (*capax Dei*). He described this fundamental possibility everyone has for relationship with God in terms of being "hearers of the Word." God self-discloses to us—God is the speaker—and we are the receivers, those who have the "ears to hear." Vocation in this sense is understood as our ongoing decision to respond to or ignore relationship with God.

The twentieth-century American Trappist monk Thomas Merton like-wise wrote about our respective vocations from God. On one hand, it refers to the state of life we discern according to the Holy Spirit (that is, marriage, consecrated life, single life, etc.). On the other hand, it includes an even more particular call to be who it is that God created each of us to be. Merton called this the discovery of our true self, which can only be found in finding God.

Francis of Assisi recognized the universality of vocation and the particu-larity of our identities when he wrote, "What we are before God, that we are and nothing more [or less]" (Admonition XIX). To discover our truest purpose and meaning, to hear our ultimate calling (*vocare* in Latin—that's where "vocation" comes from), we must learn to see ourselves and others with the eyes of God. Only then will we come to a fuller understanding of what God has in store for us.

Any year is an ideal time for reflecting on the spirituality, meaning, and future of consecrated life, and it is always important to recall how our sense of vocation serves as the starting point for all such consideration. In a world that is becoming increasingly louder with distractions vying for our attention, learning to hear the Word, being open to the stirrings of the Spirit, and coming to develop our relationship with God more intimately is more challenging. Women and men who embrace religious life—like those people who faithfully commit to other states of life—witness to the world the possibility of hearing the Word and living the call in a particular way. All of our vows matter.

THE SECOND VATICAN COUNCIL'S DECREE on the renewal of religious life spends a lot of time highlighting how we might today embrace the evangelical counsels of poverty, chastity, and obedience that we are called to profess. Yet, I believe that in reflecting on the spirituality and meaning of consecrated religious life in the world today, we must also explore the evangelical qualities that we are called to express. In other words, Vatican II outlined the basic principles of how religious life should be lived today, but I want to encourage us to consider just how religious life should look today. And this is not just something reserved for women and men religious, but for all Christians who, by virtue of their baptismal promises, have vowed to live the Gospel in whatever walk of life they find themselves.

There are many evangelical qualities of religious life to explore, and I hope to examine many of them here and in the chapters that follow. To begin, I invite you to join me in considering how we are called to express the evangelical quality of foolishness.

Being foolish has deep scriptural roots. For example, St. Paul in his First Letter to the Corinthians opens with a reflection on the seemingly absurd claim Christians profess in preaching Christ crucified. To preach the life, death, and resurrection of Jesus was a *skandalon*—a stumbling block—for Paul's Jewish brothers and sisters, and it was complete foolishness to those imbued with Hellenistic ways of thinking. At its core, Paul's introductory message is a challenge for his hearers to reorient their compasses, to reboot their hermeneutical lenses, to change their gears.

Paul goes on in his letter to challenge the Corinthians on the ways social injustices had begun to creep into the celebration of the Lord's Supper, on the ways that the system of haves and have-nots had begun to spoil the "one bread" and begun to maim the "one body," on the ways that maintaining the "order of the world" had begun to supplant living in the reign of God. At first glance, it can seem like a standard binary of good and bad. But it's not that simple. It is not the world as such that is the problem, but the so-called wisdom of the world. It is the logic of order, rationality, and reason that discriminates and evaluates rather than reconciles and heals. It is this way of being in the world that Jesus came to set ablaze. It is this worldly wisdom that God has made foolish.

In a world that is increasingly unjust and unequal, embracing the wisdom of God, standing up against wrongdoing, and appearing foolish offers a prophetic witness to human dignity and God's preferential option for the poor.

Today, Pope Francis offers us an inspiring example of how we are called to become fools for God. The Bishop of Rome is as foolish as they come, in all the best ways! Embracing this evangelical quality of foolishness, he is foolish with his time, foolish with his health, foolish with his security, foolish with his words, foolish with his mercy, and foolish with his love.

According to the logic of the world, a pope should be more mindful of important international matters and not so concerned about the everyday needs or problems of unknown single mothers, imprisoned young adults, visitors at his weekly audiences, and the poor around the globe. According to the logic of the world, a pope should be more careful to take it easy, especially as he continues to age and weaken in health. According to the logic of the world, a pope should be careful not to take too many unnecessary risks, unplanned detours while traveling, and always be mindful of his security detail. According to the logic of the world, a pope must toe the line, set the pace, be clear about who is in and who is out, and judge discerningly for the sake of the church.

But Pope Francis preaches Christ crucified—preaches both in word and in deed—and proclaims instead: "Who am I to judge?" Which is a stumbling block to some and utter foolishness to others.

So I think we should listen to St. Paul and consider our call to be better disciples, revealing to the world by our lives of evangelical foolishness which wisdom we embrace. May we risk boldly that which might seem absurd to the world so that the only scandal we put before others is that of the generosity of loving one another as God has loved us in Christ.

OFTENTIMES THOSE WHO ARE NOT VERY familiar with consecrated religious life or even those who may be discerning a call to it have a perception that what is required of Gospel living requires an absolute break with the rest of the world. This fleeing the world, what the desert fathers and mothers called *fuga mundi* in the first centuries of monasticism, is emphasized at times by women and men who view the world as a place of temptation, a sinful context for Christian living, a landscape of distraction and perhaps even evil.

It can be comforting to imagine oneself as so committed to the Christian life, to following God's will, that participating in society and associating with others is something to be despised. It can be simpler to set off alone, apart from distractions and pressures, distant from the needs and wants and demands of others. That goes for people in all states of life. How tempting it is to want to run away, to flee the challenges of our day, and seek a simpler life and time.

But Jesus, time after time in the Gospels, makes it clear that God wants none of this from us. Take, for example, John 17:13–19, in which Jesus prays to the Father for his followers who "do not belong to the world" but, like Jesus, have been "sent into the world." Like the Lord, women and men of faith are called not to be of the world but nevertheless to remain in the world. This tension can be difficult to embrace. But it is within this tension that all Christians are called to live, and it is this particular type of worldliness that I believe is an evangelical quality of religious life that we need to express today.

Jesus came into the world, lived in the world, engaged with all people in the world, ate and drank and laughed and loved in the world. Yet he was not part of what so many in his own time thought being in the world meant. The world, as St. Paul writes at the beginning of his First Letter to the Corinthians and as we reflected on in the last chapter, is shorthand for talking about a logic and wisdom that is purely of human making. It is a way of viewing people and creation according to the standards established by those who hold and seek to maintain power and social status.

Whereas the world says some people are unlovable, some actions are unforgiveable, and some are more important and have greater value than others, God in Christ Jesus says to us that all people must love as they have been loved, all must forgive as they have been forgiven, and in the eyes of God, everyone has intrinsic and inalienable dignity and value.

To be of the world is to embrace a creed of human logic and order; to be in the world like Jesus Christ is to profess faith in a God that turns those standards upside down. It is about taking the evangelical quality of foolishness that we already explored and applying it to real life!

But what does this look like in practice? For that, I suggest St. Francis and Thomas Merton offer us two great models. Francis's form of life sought at all times to break down barriers to relationship in his thirteenth-century context. He wanted his followers, lay women and men as well as friars and sisters, to be among those in the world, not hidden away in a monastery, secure and comfortable. He took this call of worldliness very literally. Similarly, Merton lived a monastic life, seemingly fleeing the world behind the cloister walls of his abbey in twentieth-century Kentucky. Yet in time, he came to realize that to be a Christian meant engaging with people outside those walls through his writings and correspondence. It meant caring about the injustices and social inequities of the time and working for peace and justice. It meant demonstrating that even the monastic life, which seems so much on the surface like an abandoning of the world, is really another form of living the Gospel in the world.

In order to live the Christian vocation today, we must be a missionary people, a certain kind of worldly people, a people who take seriously the joys and hopes, the griefs and anxieties of all women and men with us in the world.

THE RENOWNED LUTHERAN THEOLOGIAN and World War II martyr Dietrich Bonhoeffer is famous for presenting a number of helpful ways to look at Christian discipleship. I believe that among the most significant for those of us in religious life today, or living out our vows in any walk of life today, is that of the distinction between "cheap grace" and "costly grace," discussed in Bonhoeffer's book *The Cost of Discipleship*.

Bonhoeffer wrote that "cheap grace is grace without discipleship, grace without the cross, grace without Jesus Christ." Meanwhile, "costly grace confronts us as a gracious call to follow Jesus, it comes as a word of forgiveness to the broken spirit and the contrite heart. It is costly because it compels a man [or woman] to submit to the yoke of Christ and follow him."[1]

There is a lot of cheap grace floating around. It doesn't always appear so clearly labeled. It seems to me that one of its most common iterations comes in the form of the not-quite-exhortative exhortation, "God wants you to be happy!" This is a type of cheap grace, an untruth that has little to do with Christianity, the Gospel, Jesus Christ, and therefore, little to do with religious life.

God does not want us to be happy any more than God wants us to be sad or nervous or tired or anxious. Happiness is fleeting; it's ephemeral. It's a feeling and emotion that at its core is certainly good, or at least neutral, like all human feelings—and like the full range of human emotions, happiness comes and goes. And that's OK.

However, we're often told, even by religious leaders, that happiness is what we should strive after in making life choices. Instead, Jesus desires for us not to be happy but to have joy, and to have it completely.

I believe that we are called to live the Gospel value of joyfulness, which is an evangelical quality made all the more timely in the wake of Pope Francis's apostolic exhortation *Evangelii Gaudium* ("The Joy of the Gospel"). As those who have professed the evangelical counsels and prioritize the Gospel

---

1. Dietrich Bonhoeffer, *The Cost of Dsicipleship* (New York: Simon and Schuster, 1995), 45.

as our blueprint for life, our task is to express that quality of evangelical joyfulness within our communities so that what we encounter in our own experience of a kind of domestic church can carry over into our ministerial life with others.

Evangelical joyfulness is simply another way to call the experience of living with compassion, kindness, humility, meekness, patience, forgiveness, love, and thanksgiving. These are the dispositions that Pope Francis identifies throughout *Evangelii Gaudium* as characteristic of the true life of discipleship. Which is, of course, a lot easier said than done; a lot more comfortably discussed, than lived.

Pope Francis writes:

> The great danger in today's world, pervaded as it is by consumerism, is the desolation and anguish born of a complacent yet covetous heart, the feverish pursuit of frivolous pleasures, and a blunted conscience. Whenever our interior life becomes caught up in its own interests and concerns, there is no longer room for others, no place for the poor. God's voice is no longer heard, the quiet joy of God's love is no longer felt, and the desire to do good fades. This is very real danger for believers too. Many fall prey to it, and end up resentful, angry, and listless (2).

The great danger that Pope Francis is naming here is that cheap grace, as Bonhoeffer put it, a striving after the individualistic and fleeting happiness so many think God wants us to have. When that cheap grace grows tired and cold, when that happiness is never perpetually sustained, then what?

Pope Francis anticipates this when he notes that "there are Christians whose lives seem like Lent without Easter," and I believe that this can so often be the case for men and women religious. So may we, in whatever we do, in word or deed, do in the name of the Lord Jesus, giving thanks to God through him, and in turn, express to our brothers and sisters, in community and in the world, the evangelical quality of true joyfulness.

WE ARE THE SALT OF THE EARTH. We are the light of the world. But do we really understand the significance of these descriptions from the Gospel? I know that I often don't.

Many of us hear the passage from Matthew's Gospel about being the salt of the earth and think about the way that salt can be used to add some flavor to food. It is often seen as an optional ingredient included alongside pepper on the dining table, something that spices things up and increases flavor. Or it is seen as optional but from the opposite vantage point—as an ingredient to be avoided because too much gives one high blood pressure.

However, when the human body doesn't have the right amount of sodium—of salt—bad things happen. Without it, the electrical systems that communicate important messages from our brains to all the vital parts of our bodies shut down. Lack of salt can also kill us.

From this perspective, the description of you and me as salt takes on another level of metaphorical value. If as Christian disciples you and I are salt, then we are not simply optional, but absolutely necessary. If we are salt, then each of us is required for the healthy functioning of the Church, which is the Body of Christ. And here we come to another evangelical quality of religious life that I'd like to share with you: evangelical bodiliness.

To embrace Gospel bodiliness is to remember our truest identity as members of the Body of Christ brought into new relationship with God and one another through baptism.

As men and women committed to our respective vows of discipleship and to the religious life or marriage, we need to be especially cautious not to allow positions of authority, praise from others, signs of well-meaning respect or honor distract us from how we should see ourselves, especially as we relate to others.

I am reminded of what St. Francis of Assisi said to his brother friars as recorded in Admonition XIX. During a pastoral visit to a friary, he famously instructed his confreres that, despite their increasing smugness resulting from being well received, "What you are before God, that you are and nothing more."

It can be easy to forget this, and to see ourselves as more important, more significant, different or set apart from others. Though marriage is a sacrament and a gift from God, it is just one way of being in the world. Though the single life is indeed its own form of committed discipleship, it is no better than another state of life. Though professed religious life is distinct, it is just one among many ways to live one's Christian vocation born in the waters of baptism!

To be salt of the earth is to remember what St. Augustine instructed his catechumens on the celebration of the Eucharist: "See who you are and become what you see!" We are to see that we are the Body of Christ. Likewise, Vatican II's *Sacrosanctum Concilium* ("Constitution on the Sacred Liturgy") teaches that Christ is made present not only in the Eucharistic species, but also in the Word and in the members of the assembly including the presider.

To be salt of the earth is to remember that our principle identity and vocation is to be a disciple, and this comes long before and remains long after being a consecrated religious or an ordained presbyter or someone in a position of familial or societal leadership. God does not care what title or position or influence we have. If he did, Christ might have said: "The first shall be best, and the last, well they're not as important." It seems to me that the Gospel continually challenges us to remember that it's how we relate to all we meet in whatever state of life we find ourselves that truly matters.

When you and I someday embrace our "sister bodily death," as St. Francis put it, we will stand before the Lord the same as we did on the day of our baptism, with no titles and accomplishments, no Roman collars or religious habits or business suits with corporate prestige to hide behind. All we'll have is how we related to God in relating to others. To be salt of the earth is to prioritize and value the communion we share with one another. It is to remember that we are all essential and necessary for the full, healthy functioning of the Body of Christ, just as the human body needs salt to live well. It is to know that Christian discipleship is not optional or reserved for those with a particular taste for it, but is required for all the baptized.

According to the popular imagination and the way in which we frequently discuss it, the image that a prophet conjures up is typically one who is able to predict the future, foresee coming events, or correctly guess the outcome of some sporting event. However, being a real prophet has nothing to do with being a fortune-teller and everything to do with seeing the world as it really is.

The reason it is important for us to take a closer look at what it means to be a prophet is that among the many other evangelical qualities required for those of us living vowed lives and those committed to following the Gospel today stands the need to embrace and express a prophetic voice. Talk of being prophets in the world is commonplace among us, but it has been my experience in talking with people from around the world that a rich understanding of what constitutes the prophetic voice remains unclear.

When we examine the Old Testament, a clearer picture of what a true prophet looks like begins to emerge. They are people who are almost always hesitant to accept the call from the Lord. They are oftentimes nervous and concerned about their safety, aware of course that to be a prophet will come with some real-life consequences. It has always been a little comforting to me that Jeremiah, Jonah, Moses, and others were so reticent. I can certainly relate to this dimension of our universal baptismal vocation (we are, after all, each baptized into the threefold character of Christ as priests, prophets, and kings). The reason that being a prophet is such risky business is that it requires speaking truth to power, which is bound to upset those in control.

Speaking the truth isn't something determined by the prophet on his or her own, but rather is a command that comes from God. The truth doesn't appear as if it were a text message or e-mail sent down from above, but instead arises from the disconnection the prophet recognizes between the vision God has for humanity and creation and the way things are in fact playing out in history. How does one come to know God's vision? The answer is scripture. A prophet must become immersed in revelation, be open to the Spirit's inspiration, and allow the narrative of God's saving love in salvation history to inform his or her whole outlook.

God's vision for human flourishing is encapsulated in the ministry of Jesus wherever the Lord embraces those who have been abused by the powerful, scorned by the self-righteous, or pushed to the margins. Jesus calls for each person to be his brother's keeper, to love others as she has been loved by Christ, to serve the least among us and in so doing serve God. Yet, what was happening then and continues today is the disregarding of the others, the abuse of the powerless, the abandonment of the poor, and the violence among people and between nations.

God's vision for the whole of creation also is oriented toward harmony and peace. It is illustrated when the lion lies down with the lamb and when human beings remember their true place within the community of creation as brother and sister, and not as one above creation as some kind of sovereign lord. This last point is something we'll explore further in the next chapter.

The prophetic voice is the expression of this disconnect in words and actions, calling people of faith as well as others of good will to return to God and live in a new way. We must follow in the footsteps of the prophets that have come before, reminding those in power that God has revealed to us in scripture that we must always think of the poor and forgotten first, to care for the least among us, and to bring all the marginalized back into the fold. The prophetic voice is a witness to the world that living the Gospel is indeed possible. The prophetic voice is a confirmation that God does indeed "hear the cry of the poor" (Psalm 34) and calls all people to hear that cry and then do something concrete in response. The prophetic voice is a description of how we fall short of God's vision for the world, but it is not too late to turn back, to reach out, and to make a difference.

If we're honest, we think about ourselves all the time. According to the book of Genesis, we have been doing so ever since the Garden of Eden. But while it is certainly not good to focus on one's self individually—in other words, to be selfish—it's also not especially good to think only about ourselves collectively, as human beings. There is more.

We often overlook the fact that, in Genesis, nestled in the chapter immediately preceding the classic tale of snakes and apples and fig leaves, right there in chapter 2, is an explanation of how we human beings were fashioned by God *ha-adamah*, which in Hebrew means "from the earth." Put another way, human beings—like stones and flies and birds and dogs—are made of the same organic stuff as everything else in the cosmos.

The carbon, oxygen, hydrogen, and other elements that form the molecules that compose our bodies are the same elements that form everything else in the universe. Even that which builds the proteins according to which our DNA is encoded is shared with God's other creatures, those to whom we are intrinsically related, and those with whom we are called to be in familial relationship.

But are we?

If the travail of creation and the environmental crises of our planet are any indication, then the answer is a resounding "no." Our human-focused attitudes of exploitation and collective self-centeredness have blinded us to the inherent relationship we all have with the rest of creation. There are many reasons why this may be the case.

One reason we remain blind to our relationship with the rest of creation is that we consider ourselves superior to other animals and aspects of creation. We don't listen to either scripture or science, both of which affirm our interrelatedness and interdependence, and instead assert that categories of our making (such as rationality or language or so on) designate us as wholly other and above the rest of creation.

Another reason we remain blind is our misunderstanding of Genesis 1:26–28, in which we claim to read that we have been given "dominion" over and a mandate to "subdue" the rest of creation. Superficially, this seems like scriptural justification for a carte blanche attitude toward how we relate to the rest of creation. We've convinced ourselves that the rest of the cosmos was created solely for human benefit and that we can mine, pollute, hunt, modify, deforest, and otherwise use the earth and its inhabitants as we please.

A third reason we remain blind is our belief that we are all that God really cares about. The hubris of our perceived self-importance has led us to disregard the intrinsic value that all creation has before its Creator, as well as the intrinsic relationship everything in the universe already has with God.

As we live out our Christian vows, we have an obligation not only to be prophets calling people to care for their human sisters and brothers at the margins, but to cry out in an exhortative plea for Christians and all people of good will to care for the rest of the family of creation. Pope Francis, evoking the spirit and wisdom of his namesake St. Francis of Assisi, has time and again mentioned our obligation to the rest of creation (above all, *Laudato Si'* makes this crystal clear).

We should care for all living creatures just as we would for the wounded and threatened human persons in our own neighborhoods and families. We should look to see where our human-centered focus has led us to ignore the cry of the earth and respond with action and advocacy. We must begin with ourselves, recommitting to the Gospel life of love and service by widening the horizon of our family to include the trees that give us the air we breathe, the water that sustains our lives, the plants and animals that nourish us, and so many of the seen and unseen aspects of the community of creation we simply take for granted. After taking that step of personal Gospel renewal, we can then go forward to call others to recall that we are not just stewards or guardians, but true siblings of the earth that share a common source as creatures loved into existence by God.

Among the many gifts that the Franciscan theological tradition has given the world is Bonaventure's understanding that all creation bears a vestige of the Creator. *Vestige* comes from the Latin *vestigio* meaning "footprint." Bonaventure means that each aspect of creation somehow bears an imprint or trace of the Trinity. When we move from the self-centeredness of sin, according to which we can see nothing other than ourselves, toward a mystical awareness of contemplation, according to which we are able to see the world as it really is, we shall begin to recognize the loving presence of our creating and sustaining God in all things. In this way, we can start experiencing the whole world around us with a new sense of awe and wonder.

We might remind ourselves to take special care considering the ways in which we cultivate awe and wonder in our daily lives. We cannot give what we do not have, which means that we are first called to open our eyes to the presence of the Creator reflected in all aspects of the world around us. This takes place in a multitude of ways.

There are ways that cultivating a sense of awe and wonder can be easily done. For those who enjoy the beauty of the mountains or oceans, of open spaces and wilderness, recognizing the majesty of the Creator reflected in creation comes as almost second nature. Growing up amid the beauty of the Adirondack Mountain foothills, the serenity and grandeur of mountains, rivers, and trees has always inspired in me a deep sense of the divine. Even to this day, while driving through the hills and valleys of upstate New York, my breath can be taken away by the sight following a turn in the road, which might suddenly reveal a tree-covered mountain cast against the bluest of backdrops. For some, it may not be the outdoors, but the same can be said about the love of friends and family. When our relationships are joyful, peaceful, and supportive, it can be easy to reflect on our lives with the awe of faith and the wonder of hope.

Yet, there are also ways in which cultivating these senses is not always easy. We live in a world that suffers the effects of our sinfulness— individually and collectively—which shades the lenses through which we view the world around us with a hue of grief and the shadow of anxiety. When we consider the devastating effects human activity has wrought in terms of global climate change, when we examine the suffering of the poor and marginalized at the hands of the rich and powerful, and when we recognize that our own selfishness stands at the heart of judgment and exclusion, it is difficult, if not seemingly impossible, to witness what poet Gerard Manley Hopkins calls "the grandeur of God."

Though I grew up in a small city not far from one of the largest state parks in the country, I have since spent most of my life in large East Coast cities. Most recently, I lived for years in downtown Boston, which is without a doubt one of my favorite big cities. But still, I find myself struggling often to cultivate a sense of awe and wonder. Traffic, poverty, violence, political infighting, and so many other realities of everyday life can pull me away from God's presence in and among the noise. I can become discouraged. I can be overly distracted. I can too easily forget what the Psalms confirm for us, that "God is in the midst of the city" (Psalm 46:5).

Those of us living vowed Christian lives have many of the same problems that everyone else in the world has. For example, the propensity to over-work and be increasingly busy can prohibit us from cultivating senses that perceive the awesomeness of God. And if we cannot develop this disposi-tion, how can we expect our sisters and brothers to do so, when their work, families, and societal obligations weigh on their time and energy all the more?

Francis of Assisi, whose own life and writings inspired Bonaventure's, was understood to be a mystic. He intuited what theologians would only later expressly articulate; namely, that we belong to a cosmic family that is lovingly created, sustained by, and united to God. When he was a young man, he did not so much live a life of grave sin and disgrace, as he and his early biographers would have us believe. Rather, Bonaventure tells us that young Francis lived a life of ignorance and self-interest. This is too often our experience. Though generally good people, we overlook what is right before us: the needs of others, the beauty of creation, and the pres-ence of the Creator Spirit among us. Francis's conversion was a continual movement toward a mysticism that saw the whole world with new eyes filled with awe and wonder. Those drawn to Francis's way of life were likely attracted to this aspect of his character, for he had become a man who saw the vestiges of God all around him.

May we, may I (please God help me), work to cultivate a sense of awe and wonder in our lives. By seeing the world in this way, we begin to see things as they truly are!

It is interesting to consider how many parishes, religious institutions, and church organizations claim on signs that, in their respective spaces, "All Are Welcome." While the announcement of such a claim may vary depending on one's location around the world, in North America and especially in the United States, seeing this expression is a very common phenomenon. This is certainly a positive gesture, which represents what appears to be a genuine intention to live the Gospel in a welcoming community.

However, at times I wonder how honest those signs and banners proclaiming, "All Are Welcome," really are in these communities. Having heard certain homilies, lectures, bulletin announcements, extemporaneous comments, and other contrary messages coming from church leaders and ministers, I have to ask myself: "Are all really welcome here?"

Sure, those who seem by all outward and public appearances to be Catholic Christians of good standing (whatever that means) are undoubtedly welcome in these houses of worship and centers of learning, but what about those not so accustomed to darken the doorway of a church? What about those who have been marginalized or vilified, forgotten or abused, ignored or maltreated?

What about those whose sexual orientation does not align well with a moral theology grounded in thirteenth-century natural-law theory?

What about those who are living together unwed or are single parents or are divorced and remarried in a civil ceremony?

What about those whose employment differs in taste or lacks the propriety with which most church congregants are familiar?

What about politicians, local leaders, or community activists with whom a majority of the congregation disagrees?

What about visitors from other Christian denominations or from different faiths or from no faith tradition whatsoever?

Are all of these people welcome in our communities? They should be.

It is always fitting to consider the ways in which those in consecrated religious life, and those who live by any vows of Christian commitment, to embrace or reject the call to be women and men of mercy.

The spirit of the announcement that "All Are Welcome" is in line with so many of the respective charisms of our different religious communities, each of which has been such a gift to the whole church. For example, one immediately thinks of the famous instruction in the Rule of St. Benedict, "Let all guests who come to the monastery be welcomed as Christ Himself" (chapter 53). Or, in the Earlier Rule (1221) of St. Francis of Assisi, we are told that when the brothers encounter people different from them, those of other religions or of no faith tradition at all, they are "not to engage in arguments or disputes but be subject to every human creature for God's sake and to acknowledge that they are Christians" (chapter 16).

But the most important source of this call for us to be mercifully inclusive, hospitable, and welcoming is found in the teaching, preaching, and lived example of Jesus Christ himself. Nowhere in the Gospels do we ever have an instance of Jesus willfully excluding those that his society, religion, or culture deemed unacceptable. On the contrary, Jesus goes to great lengths to demonstrate that all are indeed welcome in his presence, especially those people others view as sinners. At the risk of his own marginalization, Jesus dines with, talks to, and even touches those whom the religious leaders of his day would have considered very unwelcome in their worshipping communities. Yet, the model Jesus places before all his followers is to walk in his footprints and extend a welcoming hand to all.

Pope Francis emphasized precisely this dimension of the Christian vocation to follow Christ in *Evangelii Gaudium*. Highlighting how accessible Jesus was to all, the pope reminds us that, "Moved by his example, we want to enter fully into the fabric of society, sharing the lives of all, listening to their concerns, helping them materially and spiritually in their needs, rejoicing with those who rejoice, weeping with those who weep; arm in arm with others, we are committed to building a new world" (269). Indeed, the new world we seek to build should be one that prioritizes communities of inclusion, modeling our lives after the example of Jesus Christ, helping to usher in the kingdom where all are welcome.

MANY PEOPLE FOCUS ON CHARACTERISTICS such as voluntary poverty or care for creation when considering the life and model of St. Francis of Assisi. I often wish that, just as regularly, they would notice the theme of mercy that frequently appears in his writing. This is a theme that has become even more important as Pope Francis has dedicated much of his teaching and ministry to showing the compassionate and merciful face of God in the world.

So important was this theme in Francis's own conversion experience that he recalls the mercy he was able to show lepers as a key turning point for him. He opens his deathbed Testament with that recollection:

> The Lord gave me, Brother Francis, thus to begin doing penance in this way: for when I was in sin, it seemed too bitter for me to see lepers. And the Lord Himself led me among them and I showed mercy to them. And when I left them, what had seemed bitter to me was turned into sweetness of soul and body. And afterwards I delayed a little and left the world (Testament, 1:1–3).

While he previously embraced his social privilege to shun and despise the lepers and poor of his day, Francis came to discover the mercy of God in his own life alongside the showing of mercy to those whom he had earlier considered the least in society.

Mercy is one of the most central elements of Christian discipleship because it always begins with God's unconditional love for each of us. In Francis's life, the central place of mercy was not limited to his own conversion. He insisted that those who sought to live consecrated religious profession according to his "form of life" (*forma vitae*) would also adopt this sense of mercy in relating to one another. This was especially important for those who were placed in positions of responsibility and leadership within the community.

In one of the most profound passages from the writings of Francis, we see the *poverello* counsel a friar who had written to him for advice in dealing with another brother. Francis makes clear what the primary focus and priority of the minister should be:

> I wish to know in this way if you love the Lord and me, His servant and yours: that there is not any brother in the world who has sinned—however much he could have sinned—who, after he has looked into your eyes, would ever depart without your mercy, if he is looking for mercy. And if he were not looking for mercy, you would ask him if he wants mercy (Letter to a Minister, 9–10).

It can be especially difficult in religious life to remember the importance of mercy in our interactions with one another. There is, of course, the close proximity in which we usually live with each other and share together in the life of community and ministry. This is equally true for those who are called to marriage and family life, as well as those who may live in some other form of intentional community. It may become difficult to step back and see each person apart from the little annoyances and habits that drive us crazy. Additionally, we Christians are conditioned by the broader culture and society as much as anybody else. This logic of the world does not often consider mercy a value, but a weakness. Therefore, so-called blind justice or the mentality of an eye for an eye approach toward others tends to govern our interactions with those who have offended, hurt, or simply annoyed us.

But Francis of Assisi calls us to resist that temptation, to see those within and outside our religious communities not according to this logic of the world, but with the eyes of Jesus Christ who has called us to show mercy in the way mercy has been shown to each of us. For Francis, mercy wasn't just an action or disposition, but the last and highest name for God. Written near the end of his life and said to be inspired by the ninety-nine names of God in Islam, Francis's The Praises of God concludes with the line: "You are all our sweetness, You are our eternal life: Great and wonderful Lord, Almighty God, Merciful Savior." In other words, the mercy of St. Francis is more than treating one another well; it is about living in a way more like God.

THAT POPE FRANCIS PROMULGATED A YEAR in which the Church focuses on mercy immediately following a year dedicated to consecrated religious life should have come as no surprise given the intersection of these two themes in nearly every address he made to women and men who profess to live the Gospel. These two themes appeared together frequently in the Holy Father's remarks and homilies during his recent pastoral visit to the United States, and they remain a touchstone of his regular catechetical teaching. Even in his second homily delivered after his election as pope, he highlighted the importance of mercy, saying: "The message of Jesus is mercy. For me, and I say this with humility, it is the Lord's strongest message."[1]

The intersection of the themes of religious life and mercy should be even clearer for those of us who commit to living the Franciscan charism in the modern world, for mercy was a theme close to Francis of Assisi's heart. And while it is important to remember the many ways that we are called to be merciful in our thoughts and in our words, we should not lose sight of the ways we are called to act with mercy in concrete and physical ways, too.

This is where the list commonly referred to as the corporal works of mercy could prove helpful for Franciscan-hearted women and men. Largely drawn from the famous final judgment scene in Matthew 25:34–40, where Jesus explains to his disciples that what is required to enter the kingdom of heaven is caring for the least of your brothers and sisters, the corporal works of mercy include feeding the hungry, giving drink to the thirsty, clothing the naked, sheltering the homeless, visiting the sick, visiting the imprisoned, and burying the dead. Traditionally, the last of the corporal works of mercy is attributed to the book of Tobit, in which the book's namesake is exiled for his merciful works, including burying dead criminals.

All seven of these concrete actions fulfill the obligation we hear about in the Letter of James to be "doers of the word, and not merely hearers" (1:22). But too often, even women and men in religious life become less

---

1. Pope Francis, *The Name of God Is Mercy* (New York: Random House, 2016), ix.

inclined to be doers and more comfortable being hearers only. The history of the founding of many active communities of women religious, including the Franciscans, shows that their commitment to education, healthcare, and direct-service ministries from the beginning has shielded some of them from the lure of complacency and a withdrawal from the needs of their neighbors.

However, such has not always been the case for many Franciscan friars as their respective branches have, with some exceptions, embraced a more clerical lifestyle focused on celebrating the sacraments and offering pastoral care in parishes. Francis of Assisi's emphasis on itinerancy in the spirit of the Gospel became secondary to the perceived parochial needs of a given community. Though this is in itself not a bad thing, many Franciscan houses became less inclined to engage in the corporal works of mercy, while becoming more inclined to focus on the spiritual needs of the people in an exclusive way.

This is what Pope Francis is getting at when, in his 2013 apostolic exhortation The Joy of the Gospel, he wrote that we should model our lives of discipleship after "Christ, who became poor, and was always close to the poor and the outcast, [and who] is the basis of our concern for the integral development of society's most neglected members" (186). To those, like many of us Franciscans otherwise occupied with spiritual, academic, or other pursuits, Pope Francis calls us to return to concrete actions and move closer to our sisters and brothers.

> No one must say that they cannot be close to the poor because their own lifestyle demands more attention to other areas. This is an excuse commonly heard in academic, business or professional, and even ecclesial circles. While it is quite true that the essential vocation and mission of the lay faithful is to strive that earthly realities and all human activity may be transformed by the Gospel, none of us can think we are exempt from concern for the poor and for social justice.... I trust in the openness and readiness of all Christians, and I ask you to seek, as a community, creative ways of accepting this renewed call (201).

So perhaps it is time to return to the basics of our Christian vocation to follow the Gospel. The intersection of consecrated religious life and mercy meet when we are open to the Spirit's call to see the needs of the least among us, the ill and imprisoned, the poor and the abandoned, and do something concrete in response. May we listen to the wisdom of James in scripture calling us to live our Christian commitments by our actions, hear the exhortation of Pope Francis in his writings, and follow the example of Francis of Assisi in caring for the physical needs of our sisters and brothers in tangible, practical, corporal, ways.

Fear Is the Enemy

Thomas Merton wrote in *New Seeds of Contemplation,* "At the root of all war is fear: not so much the fear men [and women] have of one another as the fear they have of everything."[1] Merton recognized that the source of violence in our world is fear, but it is not only physical violence that can be traced back to fear. Fear is what is at the root of so many other problems. Fear is at the heart of so much sinful action or inaction. Fear is truly the enemy of discipleship.

As women and men of faith, we should pay close attention to the ways in which we respond to fear. It is natural, of course, that we become afraid from time to time. There are good reasons and instinctive responses that have developed over time to aid us in protecting others and us from very real and present dangers. However, fear can also creep up into other circumstances for which the fight or flight mechanism of our primordial selves is not really warranted.

It is no accident that one of the most common phrases to come from the mouth of Jesus Christ in the Gospels is "Do not be afraid!" In addition to the possibility that violence may emerge from our fear of others or of the unknown, fear also has the ability to incapacitate and cripple the will of individuals. Concern about things as tangible as employment or security, as well as things as ephemeral as reputation or comfort, often govern the decisions we make, the actions we take, and the relationships we develop or ignore. At so many points in the Gospels, especially after the resurrection when the disciples were particularly confused and afraid, Jesus begins his remarks with loving assurance that they have no reason to fear.

True discipleship is a scary venture. It was in the time of the Apostles and it remains so today. Discipleship, which is another way of saying that one embraces the baptismal call to follow in the footprints of Jesus Christ, requires resisting the mongering that our culture so often encourages. The messages so frequently displayed in advertisements and on television promote a culture of fear that seeks to convince women and men today that they are inadequate, unlovable, and imperfect without buying this or that product, without paying for this or that service. Advertising agencies

1. Thomas Merton, *New Seeds of Contemplation* (New York: New Directions, 1961), 112.

around the globe realize that human beings make many of their choices out of fear and capitalize on that dynamic. This has also been true in so many political and military regimes throughout human history. When individuals wish to take control and seize authority, it is to the weapon of fear that they turn, planting the seeds of insecurity and doubt into the hearts and minds of the population.

Jesus, as truly human, understood the experience of fear. Weeping in the garden on the night he was betrayed, the Lord expresses solidarity with those who face physical harm and emotional stress. But Jesus, as truly divine, also understood that following the Father's will means working to overcome the inhibitive fear that too often prevents us from doing what is right and speaking the truth when necessary. Hence, Jesus's first words to his followers—then and now—are always "Do not be afraid," because when we surrender to fear we are unable to live the Gospel.

In a 2013 homily, Pope Francis reflected on the question of fear and discipleship as portrayed in the Acts of the Apostles (5:12–42), which tells of the early disciples and their response to persecution. Pope Francis asked: "Where did the first disciples find the strength to bear this witness?" And answered that, "Their faith was based on such a strong personal experience of the dead and risen Christ that they feared nothing and no one, and even saw persecution as a cause of honor that enabled them to follow in Jesus's footsteps and to be like him, witnessing with their life."[2]

Just as Pope Francis reminds us, those called to specific vocations, and all the baptized, must turn not to worldly responses in the face of fear—to consumerism, violence, self-centeredness, and the like—but instead turn to a strong personal experience of Christ in the Spirit. Like the disciples on a boat during the storm, we too will find ourselves afraid and confused in this life. But may we reach not for the fear-mongering mentality of worldly wisdom and politics and instead reach out to Christ who shows us the way through the fear toward life and courage. Only then can we defeat the enemy of Christian discipleship, living fearlessly as witnesses of the Gospel in a world so desperately in need of that hope.

---

2. Pope Francis, *The Church of Mercy* (Chicago: Loyola, 2014), 53.

I WANT TO CONCLUDE BY SAYING A FEW words about the very foundation of religious life, the three vows that stand at the heart of this form of Gospel living: poverty, chastity, and obedience.

These three evangelical counsels are often misunderstood. They seem odd and, at times, even disconcerting. Poverty? In a capitalist, consumer-driven society where consumption is what fuels the economy, any talk of having less can appear bizarre. Chastity? There are both natural and cultural reasons why embracing voluntary chastity might appear absurd. Naturally, there is a biological drive toward connection and reproduction; culturally, much of our media and entertainment in the global West is preoccupied with sexual expression and activity. Obedience? Well, nobody likes to be told what to do!

And yet, all of these common concerns or hesitations minimize the complexity and depth of these three commitments in consecrated religious life. Poverty is not simply about having less, chastity is not simply about sexual relationships, and obedience is not simply about surrendering one's agency or control. Having a renewed sense of the deeper meaning and implications of religious vows can unveil the joy such a life can give and hope it reveals to the church and world.

Evangelical poverty, in contrast to the popular romanticizing of abject or material poverty, is not about going without or forgoing material possessions as an end in itself. Instead, the type of poverty that Jesus models in the Gospels and which Francis and Clare of Assisi champion in their vision of Christian discipleship is a poverty that serves as a means to a greater end. One is called not to an inverse arms race where religious women and men try to be poorer than the next guy because this kind of poverty is always an evil by which people go without having those basic needs met that are necessary for foundational human flourishing. Instead, we are called to divest ourselves of all things that stand in the way of relationship while also disavowing the consumerist systems that benefit a few while disenfranchising billions. The aim is then about putting others or the common good before one's own individual interests and comfort. It's about breaking down all barriers—material or internal—that separate people from authentic relationship with others.

Chastity is too often portrayed as a masochistic sacrifice, which at best is reduced to a curious ascetical practice reserved for the spiritual elite and at worst is viewed as emotionally or even physically repressive. In truth, what God calls us to in embracing a life of committed chastity is a life of love. There is nothing at all wrong about romantic love (in Greek, *eros*) nor is there anything wrong with the love of friendship and family (*philia*), but Christ in the Gospels beckons all the baptized to exercise another kind of self-offering love (*agape*). We seek to respond to Christ's call for a radically inclusive love in their profession of chastity as a way of life. Chastity is about freely choosing to forego an exclusive commitment of love for a broadly inclusive commitment to love in the spirit of Christian charity. It's not about withholding, suppressing, or denying; it's about loving in as open a way as possible.

Although the tradition within some religious communities has sometimes been more militaristic in its conception and exercise of obedience over the centuries, particularly before the reforms of the Second Vatican Council, a fuller appreciation for the evangelical counsel of obedience reveals a more nuanced dimension of religious life. Rather than the fideism of blind obedience that the religious vow tends to evoke in the popular imagination, what women and men most often profess to do is more like learning to listen than painstakingly playing Simon Says. The root word of our English word *obedience* is the Latin word *oboedire*, which is a compound word joining together the prefix *ob-* ("in the direction of") with the verb *audire* ("to hear"). Obedience is the commitment to honing one's ability to listen by training the mind, heart, and ear in order to discern God's will as expressed within the local community. It is a promise not to unthinkingly put oneself first, but instead remain open to the Spirit's work in and among the body of Christ, which is the Church.

While this reflection on the three vows of Christian living applies most proximately to the experience of women and men in consecrated religious life, there are lessons here for people in any form of vowed commitment.

Pope Francis, following the example of his namesake St. Francis, has frequently reminded the Church that evangelical poverty is a universal requirement of Gospel living. The notion of chastity, sometimes confused with clerical celibacy, is not something reserved for priests, nuns, and brothers alone. Instead, it can be a way of considering our loving way of being in the world. You might ask yourself, "Does my inclusive spirit of love, nurtured by my particular commitment to an individual in an exclusive relationship, allow me to love more like Christ in the world or not?" The vow of obedience is the same for married people as it is for those in consecrated religious life. Spouses, too, are called to listen to one another and remain open to the working of the Holy Spirit in their lives.

As we move into the future, striving to live up to the call from God that we've received, let us remember the charismatic gifts the Spirit provides to the Church in the lived example of women and men committed to Gospel life, which prioritizes relationship through evangelical poverty, seeks an inclusive form of love through chastity, and learns to listen more attentively to the voice of God present in the world.

THERE ARE MANY PEOPLE TO WHOM I wish to express my gratitude. First, I want to thank my brother friars both in my local community at St. Anthony Shrine in Boston and throughout the East Coast of the United States. In a special way, I thank Louis Canino, OFM, and David Hyman, OFM, who run St. Francis Springs Retreat Center outside Greensboro, North Carolina. They graciously welcomed me into their local community for a short time last year while I was on retreat working on this and other writing projects.

Completion of this book project took place during a particularly hectic time in my life during which I was simultaneously traveling a great degree to deliver invited lectures and lead retreats, working on my doctoral dissertation at Boston College, discerning which academic faculty position I would accept as my next ministry assignment, all the while continuing regular pastoral ministry. I am thankful for everybody who was there for me (or put up with me, as it may have been). I am especially grateful to Kevin Mullen, OFM, my minister provincial; Brian Robinette, my dissertation advisor; Kevin and Ann Marie Horan, my parents; and David Golemboski, a great friend; all of whom were instrumental in providing me with guidance, support, insight, and care during those stressful months.

I would be remiss if I didn't acknowledge Jon Sweeney, my editor, and Mark Lombard, book division director at Franciscan Media. Both Jon and Mark have been prompt in their correspondence and supportive of the idea for this project from day one. Jon has been an especially gracious editor whose edits and suggestions have certainly contributed to strengthening both the content and my voice in this book. Additionally, I thank Matt Malone, SJ, the editor in chief of *America*, for the invitation to serve as a columnist at that august publication. It has been and remains an honor to work with such talented editors and colleagues at *America*, in whose pages some of the reflections collected in this book first began. Likewise, I express my gratitude to Mary Stommes, editor of *Give Us This Day*. She remains one of the most talented editors with whom I have worked, and she is to be thanked for making some of my Scripture reflections stronger and clearer through her editorial suggestions. It was in *Give Us This Day* that some of the themes of the chapters in Part II were first explored. Finally, my thanks go to Mario Conte, OFM Conv., the executive editor, and Corrado Roeper, the editorial secretary of the English edition of *Messagero di Sant'Antonio* (Padua, Italy), whose invitation to write a series of articles on the occasion of Pope Francis's announcement of the Year for Consecrated Life led me to first reflect on some of the themes found in the last part of this book.

Finally, I dedicate this book to my dear friend and colleague Jessica Coblentz. Over the years she has been one of my best supporters and constructive critics, a person whose commitment to ministry and lived theology is exemplary, and one of the kindest and most generous people you could hope to meet. I am honored to count her among the closest people in my life and grateful for her enduring friendship.

ABOUT THE AUTHOR

Daniel P. Horan, OFM, is a Franciscan friar of Holy Name Province (New York) who teaches systematic theology at the Catholic Theological Union in Chicago, a columnist for *America*, and the author of several books, including the award-winning *The Franciscan Heart of Thomas Merton: A New Look at the Spiritual Influence on his Life, Thought, and Writing* (2014). He is the author of more than eighty popular and scholarly articles; is a frequent lecturer and retreat director around the United States, Canada, and Europe; and has previously taught theology at Siena College, St. Bonaventure University, the Catholic Theological Union (Chicago), and the School of Theology and Ministry at Boston College. Fr. Dan is the former Catholic Chaplain at Babson College in Wellesley, Massachusetts, and currently serves on the Board of Directors of the International Thomas Merton Society. The recipient of several distinctions, he was awarded an honorary doctorate of humane letters by Felician College (New Jersey) in 2015.